Ten Steps for Recording Pictographs and Petroglyphs

Ten Steps for Recording Pictographs and Petroglyphs

Methods and Technologies

Lawrence L. Loendorf
and Nancy Medaris Stone

The University of Utah Press
Salt Lake City

The Defiance House Man colophon is a registered trademark of the University of Utah Press. It is based on a four-foot-tall Ancient Puebloan pictograph (late PIII) near Glen Canyon, Utah.

Cover photos: The left photo shows a rock art panel; the right photo shows that panel enhanced by DStretch software.

Library of Congress Cataloging-in-Publication Data

Names: Loendorf, Lawrence L., author. | Stone, Nancy Medaris, author.

Title: Ten steps for recording pictographs and petroglyphs: methods and technologies / Lawrence L. Loendorf and Nancy Medaris Stone.

Description: Salt Lake City : The University of Utah Press, [2025] | Includes bibliographical references and index. |

Identifiers: LCCN 2024020299 | ISBN 9781647691905 (paperback) | ISBN 9781647691912 (ebook)

Subjects: LCSH: Petroglyphs—Research—Technological innovations. | Rock paintings—Research—Technological innovations. | Archaeology—Methodology. Classification: LCC GN799.P4 L64 2024 | DDC 709.01/1309009—dc23/eng/20240712

LC record available at https://lccn.loc.gov/2024020299

Errata and further information on this and other titles available at UofUpress.com.

Contents

Preface: Developing a Method

Where does a method come from? In the 1970s, when I first began to teach and to do archaeological fieldwork, the methodological tool kit for recording rock art was not bulging with techniques. For decades, drawings of the images found on rock surfaces, supplemented by photographs taken with film cameras, were the available procedures, so the answer to the preceding question was, then, from traditional practice.

The documentation of rock art is no longer a static pursuit but has been changed dramatically by a range of technological developments, among them Global Positioning System (GPS) instruments and digital cameras. These and other devices are now integrated with image-enhancing software, with the result that researchers can now both observe and manipulate the figures they study with informative clarity.

In 2010, I and several colleagues established a nonprofit company, Sacred Sites Research (SSR), with the primary goal of recording and protecting sacred sites that are important to Native Americans for traditional reasons. The 10-step method described in this book has emerged from the preliminary, on-site, and subsequent analytical work that SSR teams have done and continue to do. The described steps should be considered short introductions that link topics to references where more information can be obtained. As such, this book represents an approach to solving problems that SSR has encountered during the rock art recording process, and the procedures—our 10-step method—that have provided successful solutions.

The research performed by SSR teams is guided by several fundamental principles. First and foremost among them is the fact that rock art sites are archaeological sites and need to be studied in the same way as other archaeological manifestations. The soils, flora, and fauna are as essential a part of the rock art site record as they are of buried archaeological sites. Rock art sites are places where people left images on rocks, but the rock-art-making activities were embedded in patterns of living that often become apparent by an analysis of the artifacts and features discarded at a site. Sometimes the associated artifacts or features are found through excavation, but in most instances, they are recovered from site surfaces.

SSR teams have learned that it is as instructive to analyze the chipped stone debitage and ceramics at a rock art site as it is to examine the same material at a site where rock art is not present. Artifacts such as obsidian flakes from a particular obsidian source reveal the same information whether they are found at a rock art site or on a lithic scatter site: the individuals who left the debris were engaged in the same interaction spheres.

Another of SSR's guiding principles is the recognition that the overwhelming majority of North American rock art sites were produced by Native Americans. Contrary to popular ideas at various times, none of the sites were made by visitors from outer space, nor were any created by Celtic or Chinese intruders (Fell 1976; Ruskamp 2022). They are the work of Native Americans and their ancestors, and the current descendants of the Native groups that made the rock art often retain significant knowledge about the sites. While sites with Euro-American inscriptions exist, they primarily contain names, initials, and dates that contribute to the historical research associated with trails and the locations of warfare. Although the techniques described in this book apply to historic inscriptions, the emphasis is on Native rock art.

A vital principle governing SSR research emphasizes the importance of working with the Indigenous groups whose ancestors produced the rock art. My experience with Native Americans at rock art sites began in the late 1960s during the initial recording of the Hilej Pictograph site near Joliet, Montana. Hilej was on privately owned land, and the landowner reported that on more than one occasion in the prior decade a carload of "Indians" had come to his door to ask permission to visit the site. They would spend an hour or so there, and, when leaving, they would stop and thank the landowner.

When asked which tribal group the visitors represented, the landowner admitted that he did not know.

The Hilej site contains images of large shield-bearing warriors that are now classified as part of the Castle Gardens rock art style. Some of the site's distinctive imagery is similar to rock art associated with Crow and Kiowa groups, so rock art enthusiast Stuart Conner initiated an effort to determine the extent of Crow involvement. Since the Hilej site was located in prime Crow territory, he organized a trip to the site with Francis Bear Claw, Roger Stops, and Chester Medicine Crow. Chester was the youngest son of Medicine Crow, a renowned Crow warrior, and it was hoped he would have traditional knowledge about the site. I was fortunate to be included in that expedition, which occurred in June 1972.

Although Medicine Crow, Bear Claw, and Stops did not have any traditional knowledge about Hilej specifically, they explained that the Crow referred to the rock art images at the site as "ahpaláaxawaalaatuua," or ghost writing. Leaving the Hilej site, we crossed the valley to visit the Joliet site, well known for its petroglyphs of horses and riders. Upon arriving, Stops and Bear Claw almost instantly began to speak in the Crow language and then explained to me in English that the theme being illustrated was warfare. They even recognized some of the warriors based on parts of their clothing and deciphered the events depicted in the scenes. The images, they said, were known as "baáhpawaalaatuua," or rock writing, and the site was recognizably a Crow site where warriors returning from expeditions would stop to leave an account of their adventures.

Two things were apparent. One, our Crow informants recognized ghost writing and rock writing as two distinctly different kinds of rock art. And two, Native Americans have traditional knowledge about rock art, and they should be consulted whenever possible as important participants in the rock art recording process.

In the years since the visit to the Hilej and Joliet sites, I have worked at rock art sites with a dozen different Native American tribes. My experience has taught me that often it is not the knowledge they bring about the images at a site that is important. Rather, the involvement of Native American consultants during fieldwork can provide invaluable insights, overlooked by many archaeologists,

FIGURE 0.1. Chester Medicine Crow at the Hilej Pictograph site in Montana, 1972. Photograph by Stuart W. Conner. Used with permission from the Little Big Horn College Library and Archives.

about the location of associated site features such as cairns, shrines, and medicinal plants.

Demonstrating respect for the sensitivities of Native American consultants regarding their cultural heritage and patrimony is a basic principle guiding the research undertaken by SSR investigators. Many rock art panels, or locations with rock art, are considered sacred sites and/or traditional cultural properties by Native Americans, and some tribal consultants may wish to perform a prayer, blessing, or cleansing before entering a rock art site or after the field recording effort has concluded.

Underlying all the steps that constitute the method presented in this book is a commitment to the concerns of tribal representatives. Native American cultural consultants are often very busy, so arranging for individuals to visit sites during a recording session can be complicated. Fortunately, most tribes have cultural offices or tribal historical preservation officers that can help arrange for consultants to participate in a project. State historic preservation offices are often able to provide contact information for various regional tribes. If a recording project is on federal or state lands, the managing agency will almost certainly have agreements with local tribes that require consultation and coordination with any project through that agency.

Because tribal offices usually have limited travel funds, it helps immensely if a project, as well as the managing agency, can offer some support for Native consultants to visit the site. Unfunded rock art recording projects have the option of applying for small grants from groups like the American Rock Art Research Association.

If a rock art site is on private land, it is essential that the landowner be made aware if tribal members are consulting on the project or are part of the recording crew. In the experience of most SSR teams, landowners usually welcome Native views about their site.

We've stressed the importance of involving Native American communities in the recording and evaluation of rock art sites. It is equally essential that this research not only informs fellow members of the scientific community but also educates the public about the significance of rock art sites and the urgency of efforts to protect them.

Lawrence L. Loendorf

Acknowledgments

Although authors are given credit for a book's content, the writing and publishing of a manuscript is always the work of a great many individuals who help in countless ways. We are grateful to Mavis Greer and Kevin T. Jones, whose pre-publication reviews suggested important additions that we gratefully incorporated. We also thank Marvin Rowe, who reviewed and offered suggestions for improvement to the section on dating. Mark Willis did the same for the photography chapter. We also appreciate the remarks offered by Barnaby Lewis, the tribal historic preservation officer for the Gila River Indian Community.

Discussions about the 10 steps with archaeologists including Myles Miller, Tim Graves, Mark Willis, and Juan Arias were useful, as were those with dozens of colleagues, among them Cobe Chatwood, Laurie White, Greg White, Terry Moody, Karen Steelman, Margaret Berrier, and David Kaiser, who encouraged us to finish the project. We appreciate the prompt responses to inquiries about references and permissions to use photographs or illustrations from Evelyn Billo, Amanda Castañeda, Tim Bernardis, Maya Bontrager, Jean Clottes, Jon Harman, David Kaiser, Chris Loendorf, Robert Mark, Joel Nicholas, Marvin Rowe, Carolyn Obagy-Davis, Gilles Tosello, Laurie White, Greg White, and Mark Willis.

We are deeply grateful to Justin Bracken, Jessica Booth, and Susan Wegener at the University of Utah Press, who shepherded our project through various levels of editorial scrutiny and close deadlines, and we send many thanks to freelance copy editor Alexis Mills for her willingness to get down into the weeds of our prose and emerge with many helpful improvements.

Larry also appreciates the support of his wife, Paula.

Introduction

Background before Foreground

A Matter of Terminology

Several decades ago, archaeologists became concerned about the appropriate collective term to use when discussing drawings and engravings on rock surfaces. Since at least the early 1960s, pictographs and petroglyphs have been referred to as rock art primarily because of their pictorial and aesthetic properties.[1] As rock art researchers began to move away from simply cataloging images based on established stylistic groups (for example, Barrier Canyon style or lower Pecos River style) to using historical and ethnographic sources to investigate the purposes that rock art might serve, the inadequacy of the term "rock art" became apparent. Questions were raised about whether, in some instances, the imagery represented spiritual messages made for their healing power and ability to transmit positive energy to the environment. This view was articulated by some contemporaneous Native Americans who believed that paintings or engravings on rock walls were not art at all but were, rather, a mechanism of communication with the sacred.

We have chosen to retain the term "rock art" even though scholarship increasingly indicates that the term does not begin to encompass

1. An early occurrence of the now widely used term "rock art" is found in Heizer and Baumhoff 1962, a work summarizing the distribution of rock art types in Nevada and eastern California and offering an analysis of their meaning.

the possible contexts in which the images were created. One reason for our decision is that the term is so deeply a part of archaeological usage that the introduction of a possibly more accurate term is problematic. Some evidence also suggests that some Native Americans think that certain North American rock drawings serve an aesthetic as well as a religious and ritualistic purpose and therefore really are art in the conventional sense of the word.

We believe that current and future research and analysis will reveal much more about the contexts in which rock art was created and the purposes it served in past societies. It will be from this knowledge base that a term to replace "rock art"—should a replacement appear necessary—will emerge.

Technical Terms

Every systematic type of endeavor, whether it is politics or plumbing, uses terms that are specific to its activities and concerns. These expressions are not in common usage because they have been invented to identify the subject matter, tools and equipment, practices, and, sometimes, the creatures being investigated and discussed. Like other scientific disciplines, rock art research has developed its own language to express the realities and concepts that it studies. Because some of the terms in this book may be unfamiliar to students of the ancient graphics represented, the more frequently used ones will be defined as we proceed.

What Is Rock Art?

The Search for Time and Meaning

Since its inception, archaeology has gradually solved many of the puzzles left to it from the past. Simply arranging the contents of the archaeological record in a reliable temporal sequence occupied many decades and a variety of techniques. Stratigraphic position was a reliable indicator of the relative age of a site's contents—except when it wasn't. Stylistic changes in artifact design and motif often suggested a progression in style from earlier to later. Known geological sequences sometimes provided a physical context with which to date the contents of sites, and in the case of associated biological material such as tree-ring sequences, artifacts and features could be correlated with years and eras.

In the late 1940s, the development of radiocarbon dating allowed archaeologists to estimate the age of objects containing organic material, resulting in considerable clarity about the time depth of cultural deposits. Archaeologists began to speak about the time frames of the in-ground deposits they excavated. The settlement sequences of localities around the world became clear, and archaeologists described coherently and reliably the movements and interactions of prehistoric peoples. Studies among contemporary peoples began to provide useful observations linking behaviors to their archaeological consequences.

The investigation of rock art, however, poses special problems. The late Rhys Jones, formerly senior archaeologist in the Department of Archaeology and Anthropology at the Australian National University in Canberra, knew this only too well from his 30 years of fieldwork in Tasmania and Australia. He described the generic experience of archaeologists excavating rockshelters almost anywhere in the world this way: "You have a cave wall which is covered in art and superpositions—there's a vast amount of detail that's there. Then at your feet you've got the sand, and for the last twenty-five years we have been digging into the sand, where we can get radiocarbon values back to forty or more thousand years. So, in the sand we have excellent chronology but very little information. And then you look at the wall above you and there's a huge amount of information, but very little chronology" (Rhys Jones, personal communication 1992).

By "information" Jones meant the beliefs and values—the complex cultural views—standing behind a parade of eight-foot-high, multicolored anthropomorphic figures or the human attitudes expressed by the tiniest wavy red ocher squiggles. Archaeologists have been eager to decode this static "information" so that it informs them about human worldviews, cosmologies, and social relations. They have needed a framework, however, for evaluating the barrage of contending claims—some well-researched and elegantly argued, others well-meaning seat-of-the-pants pronouncements—that are hurled at rock art in the hopes that some of them will stick.

We believe that rock art research is moving in the direction of providing the kind of information that Rhys Jones was eager to discover, but a systematic recording procedure using state-of-the-art techniques, coupled with knowledge of relevant ethnographic and historical data, is required to bring order, and ultimately meaning, to the universe of visual data represented by rock art. The recording process presented in this book focuses on 10 essential steps that, when followed, produce an accurate and detailed representation of the primary types of rock art that archaeologists explore on surfaces throughout the world.

Engraving and Painting

In the autumn of 1876, Col. Garrick Mallery of the United States Army was assigned to Fort Rice, a military outpost on the North American Plains located along a stretch of the upper Missouri River. He brought to this post an already well-developed interest in the graphic arts of Plains tribal peoples as well as the interest in human cultural expression that has been typical of anthropological researchers over the past two centuries.

Within six months of his assignment, Mallery published a report entitled *A Calendar of the Dakota Nation* describing a Plains Indian historical record that was made up of symbols depicting events in tribal life between 1800 and 1871. Only two months later, Mallery was asked by the secretary of the interior to permanently trade his sword and military uniform for an ethnographer's pen, notebook, and itinerant existence, and from that point on he was a full-time researcher. Traveling throughout the United States and Canada, Mallery (1886, 1893) documented the many different kinds of symbolic representation that he called "picture-writing," first in the employ of the United States Geological and Geographical Survey of the Territories and, after 1879, for the Smithsonian Institution's newly formed Bureau of Ethnology.

By "picture-writing" Mallery meant a "distinctive form of thought-writing without reference to sound" that included but was not limited to the two principal types of graphic imagery that are now identified as rock art—pictographs and petroglyphs. A distinguishing characteristic of these two types of images is that they occur exclusively in the natural landscape, usually on rock outcrops or cave walls. They differ in this significant respect from the patterns or images on portable artifacts such as ceramics or on walls of ceremonial rooms, houses, or other structures.

Petroglyphs, which are called engravings in some parts of the world, are made by pecking, incising, or abrading a rock's surface to remove the outer, dark-colored layer and expose the inner, light-colored stone. The act of pecking or incising creates a design or figure in the newly exposed stone. Usually, the more recently a petroglyph has been created, the more visible the image is. Conversely, the older a petroglyph is, the more rock varnish has developed on the surface of the design and the fainter it is likely to be.

Pictographs, or paintings, are usually made from paints composed of a source of pigment, such as clay, mixed with a liquid binding agent and applied to a rock surface with either the fingers or an applicator such as a brush. In some instances, the pigments are mixed with binders and formed into semi-hard cakes resembling crayons that are used to draw a design or figure on a rock. These two techniques—painting and using crayons—account for the vast majority of the world's rock paintings.

Sometimes the creators of pictographs smoothed the surface of the rock on which they intended to paint images, but often images were placed directly on granular, uneven sediments. Over time, exposure to wind, rain, and sun caused images to weather, although at different rates depending on the composition of the paints and the porosity and density of the rock. In Figure I.1, which shows a small portion of the large panel of images at White Shaman rockshelter in the lower Pecos River valley of Texas, some of the paint appears to be flaking, and some other substance is beginning to obscure the figures in the lower third of the photograph. In contrast, in protected settings such as Chauvet Cave in France, even though some of the painted figures are at least 30,000 years old, they remain in pristine condition. Compared to pictographs, petroglyphs are less vulnerable to natural forms of assault, but both kinds of rock art have no defenses when the defacing agent is a human being.

Other Forms of Depiction

Human inventiveness can operate at any scale, but the more massive the figure, the more awestruck the response of viewers is likely to be. Some of the largest figures—which are called geoglyphs, intaglios, or rock effigies—are those located in the Nazca Desert approximately

FIGURE I.1. Panel of paintings at the White Shaman site that shows deterioration from surface exfoliation. Photograph by Amanda Castañeda.

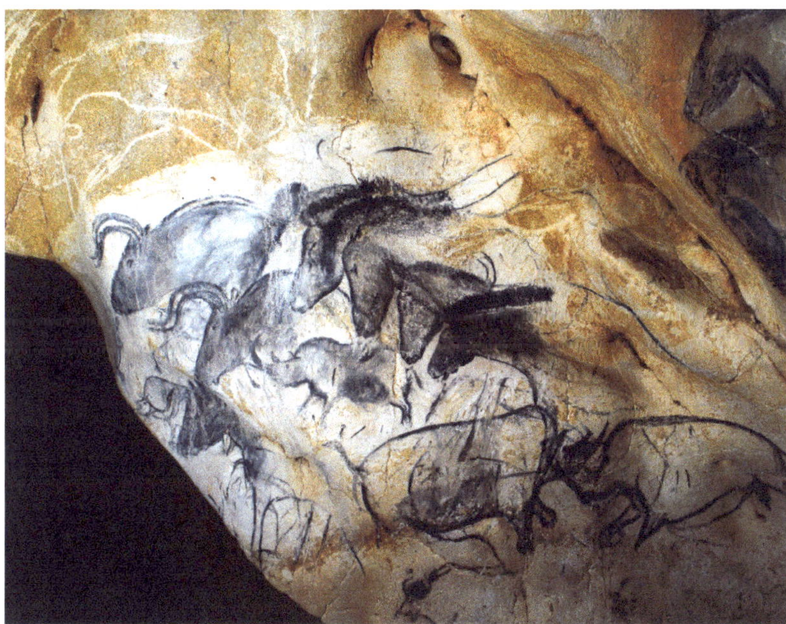

FIGURE I.2. The well-known panel of horses in Chauvet Cave is 30,000 to 32,000 years old yet looks pristine. Photograph by Jean Clottes.

400 kilometers south of Lima, Peru. There, on a high plateau that is 37 miles long and 10 miles wide, nearly 300 large figures—some of them straight lines, but others stylized animal and human-like figures—were created during the pre-Columbian era. The dark desert surface is naturally covered with iron-rich pebbles, but they were removed to create a precise pattern in the pale sediments lying beneath. Some of the straight lines at Nazca are several kilometers long, and the bird and insect figures can be the size of several football fields. The only perspective from which the Nazca geoglyphs can be appreciated in their entirety is from above, so prior to the advent of airplane travel only a few anecdotal references to these terrestrial desert phenomena were recorded.

Geoglyphs occur most frequently in arid environments where the earth's surface is exposed to little or no disturbance from wind and water. This is not to say that they were not once common features in more humid environments, only that if they were, all traces have been obliterated by water and vegetation. A notable exception, however, is the cluster of figures in chalk deposits in Wiltshire, England,

FIGURE I.3. The Uffington White Horse geoglyph, thought to date between 1380 and 550 BC. Public domain from Wikimedia Commons.

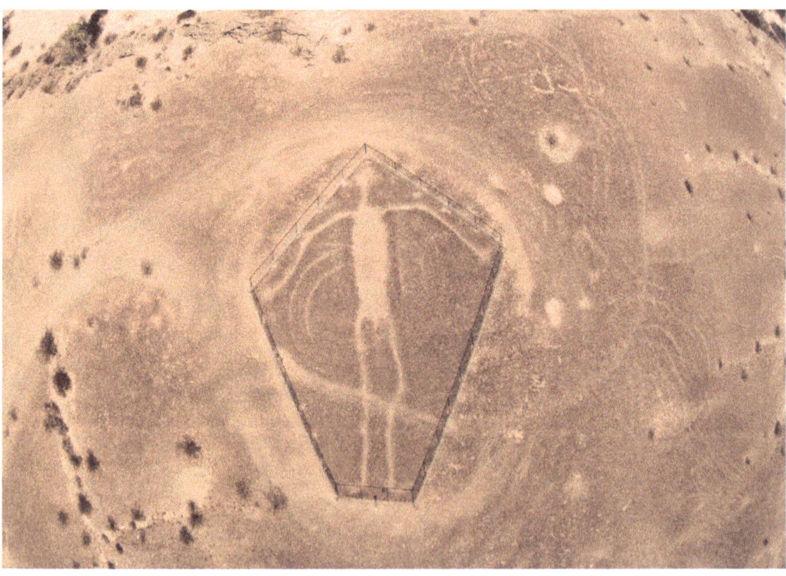

FIGURE I.4. A large geoglyph near Blythe, California. This figure and a companion figure are poorly dated but are suspected to be more than 500 years old. Public domain from Wikimedia Commons.

where the moisture in the air necessitates the frequent removal of vegetation that would otherwise obscure the images carved into the chalk. On the northern plains of North America, boulders have been arranged to reveal the outlines of large turtle figures, while the human and animal figures in the desert pavement along the Lower Colorado River, such as the so-called Bouse Fisherman in southwestern Arizona and the Blythe Giant, about 50 miles to the west in California, were made by the more usual extractive process of removing overlying pebbly sediments.

Geoglyphs have also been made by piling up soil in mounds or, in some instances, removing surface soil and replacing it with brightly colored sand or sediments. But no matter what technique has been used to create them, the question of whether geoglyphs should be classified as rock art or something else is a matter of debate. Perhaps because these figures are terrestrial phenomena, part and parcel of the sediments that archaeologists excavate, more often than not they are identified as archaeological features.

Sand paintings, made in North America by Navajos and in Asia by Tibetan lamas, are another kind of graphic image that is not included in the rock art category. Their exclusion is based on the ephemeral nature of the figures, which are created in the context of healing ceremonies and are destroyed after they have fulfilled their curative purpose.

The criterion of permanence or impermanence is not a factor in determining whether a very different kind of terrestrial construction—the medicine wheel—is or is not rock art. Found across the North American Plains, these very large structures made of boulders can be 80 feet in diameter, and like the Bighorn Medicine Wheel in Figure I.5, they appear to be calendrical devices. Important events such as the winter and summer solstices become apparent when people use the wheel's stone cairns and radiating stone spokes to direct their gaze skyward. These constructions share with other geoglyphs the fact that they were made by humans, but their function appears to be technological and not, like rock art's, expressive and communicative.

Even though geoglyphs do not fit comfortably within the category of images thought of as rock art, there are two reasons why they should not be ignored by rock art researchers. First, geoglyphs may share design features with nearby petroglyphs or pictographs, which

FIGURE I.5. The Bighorn Medicine Wheel is a prominent feature found at 9,642 feet elevation on Medicine Mountain in the Bighorn Mountains of Wyoming. Photograph by Courtney Milne, University of Saskatchewan, University Archives and Special Collections, Courtney Milne funds, #459-433.

can be an indication that the two kinds of images are contemporaneous. That stylistic similarity could prompt a researcher to attempt to date the geoglyph, and if the attempt is successful, the information could be used to establish the age of the rock art. Second, geoglyphs may also facilitate the study of rock art in instances in which there is ethnographically or archaeologically derived information about them that is relevant to an understanding of rock art.

Human Agents versus Natural Phenomena

In most instances, it is clear that rock art figures have been made by humans and that the creation of the imagery was intentional. There are examples, however, of designs on rock surfaces that were created by environmental agents, and these can sometimes be very difficult to distinguish from images made by humans. Tree branches blown by the wind, for instance, can leave marks as they repeatedly rub against a rock surface. With the passage of time, the tree may die, leaving excised lines on the rock that mimic the appearance of a humanly created linear pattern.

Water percolating from an iron-rich layer can flow across a rock face, interacting with chemical elements in the sediments to create a design that resembles a pictograph. Acid in bird dung or bat guano can dissolve a rock surface and leave marks that resemble petroglyphs. Frequently, water accumulating in surface cracks will freeze in winter, leaving deeper lines or holes when the ice thaws in spring, producing rock-art-like images.

Animals rubbing against a rock can also alter the surface and produce patterns that are sometimes confused with the product of human activity. To get rid of their itchy winter coats, North American bison, for example, often rub against the large boulders found across the northern Great Plains. In some instances, they have rubbed so intensely that large amounts of the lower portion of a boulder have been worn away. From a distance, the shapes of some of these rocks resemble the form of the bison themselves, suggesting large upper bodies often in resting positions. This resemblance has been noted by Native Americans, who sometimes have added features such as eyes and mouths to complete the transformation of the boulders into bison effigies.

The problem of determining whether a person or an animal is responsible for some kinds of images is not unique to rock art however. Archaeologists face a similar problem with several classes of artifacts and features. For instance, it is not uncommon to find a locality where there is abundant charcoal but no structures, potsherds, lithic debris, or other evidence of past human presence. In these instances, archaeologists must determine whether the burned remains were produced by a wildfire or whether they resulted from human activity. One clue to look for is the presence of a hearth. This could once have been a well-defined feature lined with stone slabs, or it could have been a more expediently produced shallow depression in which the earth was baked into a hard lining or, if the iron content of the sediments is high, turned a reddish color from the fire's heat.

As far as we know, only human beings shape, decorate, and fire clay pots and bowls, so when ceramic remains are discovered, there is no ambiguity about who created them. On the other hand, bone and chipped stone tools, or the debris left from their manufacture, can sometimes be difficult to distinguish from naturally occurring bone and stone fragments. Fortunately, there are clear-cut criteria for recognizing the difference between human tools and processed bones and the stones that have been fractured by other agents. For example, as archaeologists gain experience, they learn to look for a well-defined bulb of percussion on a stone flake, which indicates that a blow landed on a rock's striking platform, detaching the flake. But because the same kind of fractures can sometimes occur when a stone is stepped on by an animal, they might look to see if the edge of the flake was sharpened or whether other modifications were made that resulted in a partially or completely patterned artifact.

Archaeologists approach the identification of rock art in the same way. If an isolated marking on a rock is faint, or the form is ambiguous, or both, the first step is to try to eliminate all natural explanations for the mark's presence on the rock. The likelihood of the mark being a rock art image increases substantially if a search of the immediate area results in the discovery of one or more unmistakable examples of paintings or engravings of recognizable form. Once such a determination has been made, most archaeologists would not hesitate to then assign a site designation to the entire cluster of images, including the once-problematic mark.

FIGURE I.6. Bedrock metates at the Painted Grotto site, New Mexico. One of these had a high iron content not found in the surrounding rock, suggesting it was used for mixing red paint. Photograph by Evelyn Billo.

Less Well Understood Designs or Features

Archaeological sites, especially in the western United States, frequently contain other kinds of rock features such as bedrock metates, mortars, cupules, and tool grooves. Bedrock metates and mortars are normally associated with day-to-day processing of vegetable foods such as dried corn and acorns, but in some settings these features may have been used for grinding medicinal herbs or pigments. Sometimes minute quantities of the ground substance can be found on the metate surface, making it possible to determine whether the metate might have once been associated with the production of rock art. In such an instance, an archaeologist would normally record the metate, noting whether it is situated in proximity to a nearby rock art panel.

The relationship between rock art and other features such as cupules is more problematic. As their name suggests, cupules are cup-shaped depressions in the rock, normally with rounded sides and bottoms, and although there are exceptions, they are usually 5 to 10 centimeters wide and 5 to 8 centimeters deep. They can be found by the hundreds, in linear rows or haphazard patterns, across the entire surface of a boulder. Cupules are a global phenomenon, so it is not surprising that they often occur in the southeastern and western United States, including across California.

FIGURE I.7. Cupules on a boulder adjacent to a rock art site in southern New Mexico. Photograph by Mark Willis.

Because there have been very few systematic studies of cupules within the context of adjacent archaeological sites whose soil deposits have been excavated, knowledge of the context and activities associated with cupule creation is meager. A striking exception is the research of Johannes Loubser (2005) at the Yellow River site in the foothills of north-central Georgia. Loubser and his team excavated a rockshelter and midden adjacent to two cupules using the many kinds of technical analyses now characteristic of state-of-the-art excavation. The results were then evaluated in light of archaeological and ethnographic information, and a model of the behaviors producing the site was developed. The model suggests that for four centuries, small groups of hunters temporarily took shelter at the site and performed subsistence-related tasks. Loubser (2005) argues that the cupules appear to have served some sort of ritual function associated with the hunters' aspirations for a successful hunt.

Another type of enigmatic rock feature consists of complete or partial circular depressions that have a small convex nub or projection near the center. Commonly known as pecked curvilinear nucleated features, or PCNs for short, slightly more than 80 of these concavities have so far been found. They are geographically con-

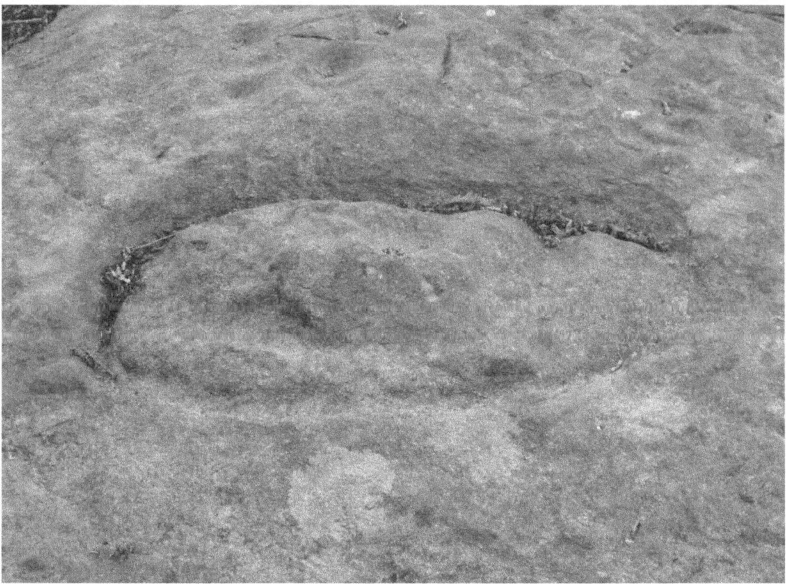

FIGURE I.8. A single pecked curvilinear nucleated feature (PCN) on the Keystone Rock in northern California. The feature, which is about 30 centimeters along its long axis, is one of many similar figures on the rock surface. Photograph by Jon Harman.

centrated in the coastal mountain ranges of California, commonly situated on serpentinite boulders that were created eons ago during episodes of movement of the earth's crustal plates. The role that PCNs played in either the practical or cosmic domains of human life has been debated; some researchers argue that they are fertility symbols, while others link them to the search for and collection of salt (Gillette 2011). Obviously, a larger sample of these features and more information about their physical context will need to be collected before definitive patterns can become apparent and a model of their function can be developed.

Whether the boundaries that define rock art can be stretched to include the phenomena known as tool grooves is an unsettled question. Found at sites across the North American Great Plains, throughout the Southwest, and in the Pacific Northwest, tool grooves are linear abraded or incised lines that are sometimes oriented in parallel rows but in other instances occur in cross-hatched patterns. They are usually less than 30 centimeters long—more often

FIGURE I.9. The Punctate site, Nevada. The drilled holes are thought to have been used to shape arrow point tips, and the grooves to shape arrow shafts. Although such functions would have been primarily utilitarian, the holes and grooves were made into interesting abstract forms. Photograph by Lawrence Loendorf.

ranging between 15 and 20 centimeters—and vary in width from 1 to 5 centimeters. They are usually less than 4 centimeters deep. One characteristic that almost all tool grooves share is their placement on sandstone outcrops, rarely if ever occurring on limestone, basalt, or other rock substrates.

There is widespread agreement that tool grooves result from the manufacture of bone, antler, and wooden artifacts. These can range from awls and knife or scraper handles to bone projectile points. Sharpening the points of wooden digging sticks may also account for some tool grooves. In archaeological circles in Colorado and Utah, however, the belief—originating with the late Barry Fell(1976)—is prevalent that many tool grooves are examples of an ancient Celtic writing system known as "Ogam." The rejection of this belief by most archaeologists is based on the fact that except for the designs in two counties in West Virginia on which the claim is based, there is no supporting archaeological evidence of the prehistoric presence of Celtic visitors to North America.

Fake or Fraudulent Rock Art

Archaeologists are frequently taken to sites or presented with images that represent attempts to imitate or replicate authentic rock art imagery. In many cases, bogus rock art can be distinguished from the real thing by the absence of surface varnish on a phony petroglyph or by the brightness of recently painted figures. But in some instances, it is very hard to determine whether a painting is a recent replica of a genuine prehistoric figure or whether it is an old image that has been altered in some way to enhance its appearance.

Examples of fakery abound. For instance, in 2005 the staff of the British Museum failed for several days to recognize the clearly fake image of "early man venturing towards the out-of-town hunting grounds" that had been hung on its walls as a prank by an artist identifying himself as Banksy.[2] Rock art researcher Polly Schaafsma (1992: 157) has recorded the efforts of Boy Scouts in New Mexico who made "look-alike" rock art images on cave walls as part of earning a merit badge. In Montana, a local sign painter was so concerned about the fading colors in the rock art at Weatherman Draw that he "enhanced" the figures using paint from his own supply (Newman and Loendorf 2005). At another Montana site, where erosion caused the partial collapse of a painted rockshelter wall, a local sheepherder painted replicas of the destroyed figures on the remaining rock so that the lost paintings would be available to future generations (Newman and Loendorf 2005). Elsewhere in the United States, a film production company on at least one occasion made paintings on cave walls and then left them in place when filming was complete (Whitley 1996).

Although the creation of fake rock art as in the preceding examples is well-known, one is left to wonder just how many other images have been augmented by people adding figures resembling actual ancient petroglyphs or pictographs to rock art panels. Faced with the task of trying to sort out the real from the fraudulent, rock art researchers

2. A sign that British Museum staff said was very similar to others in the museum states: "This finely preserved example of primitive art dates from the Post-Catatonic era. The artist responsible is known to have created a substantial body of work across South East of England under the moniker Banksymus Maximum but little else is known about him" (see "Caveman and trolley fake rocks British museum" [theage.com.au]).

FIGURE I.10. Hattie Cosgrove drawing a panel of paintings in 1928 at Picture Cave, Texas. Photograph by Burton Cosgrove.

are usually able to identify images that are poor replicas of ancient figures or that have been placed on a panel so recently that no varnish cover has developed. In the case of the well-meaning Montana sheepherder, X-ray fluorescence (XRF) identified the presence of lead in the modern paint that was used to recreate the destroyed painting, thereby verifying the contemporaneity of the fraudulent images. But as public interest in rock art increases, it is likely that more people, unaware of the cultural significance and importance of the rock art record, will be motivated to embellish (another word for this activity is "deface") or even make a mockery of the irreplaceable heritage embodied in world rock art sites. The solution to the problem lies in more effective education about the value of this fragile legacy.

Why Record Rock Art?

It's 1928, and Southwestern archaeologist Harriet "Hattie" Cosgrove is sitting on the bedrock ledge in front of a rock art panel at the site in Texas called Picture Cave. A pad of drawing paper lies on her lap, and before her is a panel of images that includes masks and so-called goggle-eyed figures. Her sketches of them, and several photographs taken by her husband, Burton, are among the few remaining representations of these ancient pictographs.

Hattie and her husband had at their command the state-of-the-art equipment used to record rock art for the next 50 years—that is, pen, paper, and a film camera. Fast-forward to the present, and to the technological innovations now available to rock art researchers. A partial list of equipment, techniques, and software would include digital cameras and notepads, GPS satellites and receivers, GigaPan tripods, unmanned aerial vehicles (drones), portable XRF analyzers, carbon 14 dating, DStretch software, and 3D modeling. Had Hattie Cosgrove been presented with this series of twenty-first-century resources, she would have been tempted to dismiss it as a baffling "word salad."

Unfortunately, at some sites and under some circumstances, the rock art documentation field session may be the only time, or the last time, that the images at a location will ever be recorded. Some of the rock art illustrated in this book has survived for thousands of years, but none of it is truly eternal. Paints and engravings erode; rock surfaces decay, spall, and crumble into cobbles and dust; and too often rock art is vandalized or destroyed by urban development. The pictographs at Picture Cave recorded by Hattie and Burt Cosgrove were missing from photographs taken in the 1960s, and their location and status remained unknown until recently.

The discovery at Harvard University's Peabody Museum of the original black-and-white photographs taken by the Cosgroves resulted in the creation of high-resolution digital copies that revealed the missing pictographs had been situated along two lower shelves of rock that were heavily fractured and unstable. Sometime between 1928 and the 1960s, the rock shelves had broken loose, fallen, and been fractured into dozens of cobbles. Apparently, the remains of the pictographs were taken from the site by looters and collectors, and all have disappeared except for a fragment found in 2011.

Today the practice of rock art documentation is complex, involving logistics, specialized techniques, an extensive range of field observations, intensive recording through drawings and photographs, and the application of modern technologies. The goal of these methods is intended to fully document rock art, including its context, surroundings, and the presence of faint or superimposed images. Determining the age and chemical composition of pigments used in rock paintings is also increasingly possible.

Given that the passage of time often results in the destruction of fragile rock art images, recording them is a matter of urgency. This book presents a systematic, scientific, and professional 10-step documentation program focusing on the instruments, techniques, and circumstances in which they are most usefully applied to the production of a virtual rock art record.

Beginning at the Beginning: Initial Investigation of a Rock Art Site

The 10 steps for recording rock art presented in this book are designed to assist individuals who have experience as archaeologists or students of archaeology recording rock art sites that are already known and have been assigned a site number. Before presenting the steps in greater detail, however, we have some guidelines for those who are the first visitors to a rock art site and are responsible for its initial documentation.

Documentation begins with paperwork. Federal agencies, military installations, and state historic preservation offices (SHPOs) have site forms that must be completed for any newly discovered or unrecorded archaeological site. These organizations also have reevaluation forms on which to record any changes at the sites when they are revisited. Tribal groups have variable rules about cultural resources and often do not rely on nontribal agencies to determine what constitutes a site. Many SHPOs and other agencies have manuals or instructions on their websites specifying how to complete the forms.

Defining the spatial boundaries of a rock art site using the criterion of the distance between images is the initial task. A common rule of thumb specifies that when two rock art images are more than 30 meters apart, two sites are present. An argument could be made, however, that when two rock art images are 35 meters apart, and no other images occur within hundreds of meters, they are part of the same site. In other words, site boundary definitions are flexible, and any questions complicating a site's delineation should be directed to the site's owner or managing agency.

When a new site is discovered, or when a previously recorded site is revisited, its location must be accurately determined. In the past, especially in the 1950s and 1960s, the maps available for locating sites were seldom accurate. Maps of the United States Forest Service and Bureau of Land Management had a scale of ½ inch to the mile, which meant that field archaeologists were happy if they could locate the site in the correct land surveying section. United States Geological Survey (USGS) maps after World War II were helpful, but good site location data were not available until the advent of GPS technology in the 1990s. For these reasons it is not uncommon to learn that the location of a previously recorded site is uncertain, making the recording of an accurate location one of the most important additions to the site record.

Important information to be recorded on an initial site form includes an estimate of the number of panels present and, if the figures are petroglyphs, whether they were incised, pecked, or abraded. Similarly, if pictographs are present, note whether they have been rendered in one or more colors. Descriptions should include all key figures as well as any available photographs. Information on the condition of the site is important, including the presence of any prominent graffiti or the obvious absence of some panels, indicating theft.

Some landowners and rock art enthusiasts who discover rock art sites are reluctant to provide their precise locations because they fear that this information will lead to vandalism. However, this assumption is incorrect because every site-recording system has mechanisms for protecting a site's location from individuals outside of the managing agency.

Obviously, collecting as much information as possible about a site during an initial visit is desirable. It is often relatively easy to record details about a small site, but recording large sites can be time consuming and beyond the scope of the inventory level. The goal in the following sections of this book is to offer avocational and professional researchers a 10-step method for recording any pictograph or petroglyph site.

STEP 1

Logistics

The accessibility of rock art sites is often problematic. While the painted or pecked surfaces originally must have been within the reach of a handheld brush or pecking tool, after a thousand or more years of erosion or burial the site may now be at the top of a crumbling talus slope or, in the case of Cosquer Cave in southern France, under 121 feet of water.

As with all archaeological projects, there are logistical issues associated with recording rock art that need to be addressed prior to entering the field. Assessing the feasibility of access to the site can be thought of as Step 1. The distance to the site from areas where vehicles can be parked is a basic concern since many rock art sites are in roadless areas requiring that recorders hike considerable distances while carrying a daunting amount of equipment. Sometimes Sacred Sites Research (SSR) archaeologists have had to wade streams and cope with snow runoff on their way to recording a site. Access to two other sites required the use of ropes and the participation of a professional climber, who visited the site in advance of the recording crew and made sure that everyone was correctly harnessed to the ropes when ascending or descending.

While permission for access to any site is essential, it is a particularly necessary step for sites on private land. Although there is currently no reason why a visitor cannot take a few photographs at sites that are managed by state and federal agencies, some public

FIGURE 1.1. Using ropes to access a site in Montana. The original access had fallen away, making it difficult for a recording crew to get up in front of the panels. Photograph by Lawrence Loendorf.

land-managing agencies now require that a prospective project director apply for a preliminary fieldwork authorization permit. The information on the application will help the manager determine whether the recording team's qualifications and methodology are compatible with the terms of the agreements the agency may have with Native American tribes or other groups with traditional ties to the site.

Equally important is a formal agreement stipulating the deliverables that the recording archaeologist will present to the site owner or manager when the project is completed. These include locational data, photographs, panel drawings, panel forms, and a site map. Whether these materials are to be submitted in digital or paper formats, as well as the time frame in which they will be produced, should be specified before recording at the site begins.

If a site has more than 8 or 10 panels, reconnaissance should occur before recording begins. During this visit, the panels can be assigned numbers, and an assessment can be made about how well on-the-ground observations correspond to the original or subsequent site descriptions. Unfortunately, the site files for most rock art

FIGURE 1.2. Pole photography is an option for recording high panels using photo-tracing techniques. Photograph by Mark Willis.

sites in North America contain incorrect or inadequate information. When SSR archaeologists record large sites, they usually find 20 to 30 percent more rock art panels than have been noted in previous site data files.

Sometimes access to the panels is more challenging than access to the site itself. Ladders or some form of lifting device will be needed

FIGURE 1.3. Archaeologists using a scaffold to record a complicated, high panel of rock paintings. Photograph by Lawrence Loendorf.

to reach high panels or ones with awkward access. Depending on the panel placement, ladders that collapse, bend, or fold into scaffold-like frames may require, as on one SSR project, the attention of a person whose only job is to pull the correct pins and slide the ladders into frames for the site recorders.

Needless to say, ropes, ladders, scaffolding, and any other equipment that might contact the rock surface are always used carefully in order to protect the rock art. SSR usually covers the top of a ladder with towels, but soft-top bumpers are available for ladders that are used extensively at a site.

In some instances, it may be possible to mount a camera on a pole, take several photos, and then photo-trace the panel later, but that limits the use of other recording techniques that require physical access to the panel surface (see "Step 3: Photographic Documentation"). On several occasions, SSR archaeologists have erected scaffolding to place the recording team in close proximity to a panel's surface. Although doing so was the most practical solution to a logistical problem, carrying the scaffolding from the vehicle to the site was labor-intensive. At one site with drive-up access, SSR recorders used a mobile raised work surface, known as a cherry picker, to move around an elevated panel surface. This lift was a cost-effective way to examine the panel and provided a close-up look at the superimposition of some of the figures that otherwise would not have been easy to detect.

Field archaeologists always confront certain environmental challenges during their work, but rock art recorders must contend with conditions that can be more problematic than those encountered during survey and excavation. The surface of dark-colored rock, for instance, can get extremely hot when in full sun, and working on these surfaces can cause heat exhaustion, heat stroke, and, in some cases, burns. Contrary to popular belief, the absence of sweating is not always an indicator of a heat-induced illness (Hawkins and Simon 2021:26), whereas dizziness, nausea, and confusion are likely symptoms.

Maintaining adequate hydration is important, but drinking only water is not always sufficient. Field crews should carry packets of powdered electrolytes in their medical kits, although simply adding salt and sugar to water is an effective antidote to dehydration (Hawkins and Simon 2021). SSR also makes certain that dill pickles are included in lunches and snacks as a way to maintain desirable levels of sodium, potassium, and magnesium.

Adequate protective clothing and sunscreen are essential for personnel recording rock art. The ability to recognize poison ivy or poison oak is necessary so that it can be avoided. Experience has demonstrated that sunburn and poison ivy are much more common among individuals working on a recording project than snakebites.

Bees, their hives, and swarms are another potential hazard for rock art recording teams. Bees are more likely to occur in rock outcrops across the southern United States, where they maintain hives in shallow caves or recesses out of direct sunlight. If hives are not directly associated with rock art panels, SSR crews mark their location with flagging tape as a warning to avoid the area. If a hive is adjacent to panels that need to be recorded, the archaeologists wear protective gear or record the panels when the temperature is low and the bees are less active. If a crew member has ever had a serious allergic reaction to bee stings, they should carry a medication like epinephrine. University and college health officials are also encouraging

FIGURE 1.4. Recording a site with an active beehive. Greg White is suited up for the task. Photograph by Laurie White.

field project directors to be trained in the emergency use of EpiPens (Hawkins and Simon 2021:24).

Insects like mosquitos can also be bothersome, so someone needs to be responsible for bringing repellent to the project site. Gnats can be the most difficult to cope with, and on some projects the recorders have had to wear netting over their faces and use tape to seal the ends of their sleeves and pants legs. On one project in a rockshelter, the gnats were so oppressive that a generator was used to power a fan and blow them away.

One of the hazards of working in and around rock formations is the presence of rattlesnakes. They do not usually pose a serious threat because they try to avoid humans, but accidental contact resulting in a snakebite can occur. A useful precaution prior to fieldwork is to find out the location and phone number of the nearest medical facility and then call to ensure that they have an adequate supply of antivenom. It is also worth emphasizing that it is wise to have a well-stocked first aid kit—and a person who is responsible for putting it into a project vehicle at the start of each recording day.

In this section we have reviewed some of the most important aspects of coordinating the complicated process of placing a team of recorders at a rock art site. It should be apparent that planning must precede all subsequent steps in the recording process. Experience has taught us that the more time that is spent on this step, the greater the likelihood that the project will be successful.

STEP 2

Identifying and Designating Panels, and Surveying the Panel Surroundings

Once a rock art site has been located and any logistical challenges have been evaluated and overcome, the first recording task is to identify the panels and associated cultural and natural features. A rock art panel is often defined as a rock surface containing pictographs and/or petroglyphs that is oriented, for the most part, in one direction—technically known as "a rock cleavage plane."

Although definitions help researchers organize the phenomena they study, reality is often more divergent and nuanced. For instance, a rock surface will often be uneven or bend slightly in ways that alter the direction of a panel, requiring the assignment of a separate panel number. It is also common for a large group of images to occur on a single panel. According to the definition, all of those images would be considered a single group even though they might not have been created as a unit. In such instances, Sacred Sites Research (SSR) recorders instead try to identify groups of related figures, each of which is assigned its own panel number. Frequently, natural cracks in the rock surface can serve as dividing lines between panels.

The goal is to be able to distinguish groups of images with similar characteristics that can be discussed as a unit in relation to, or in contrast to, other groups of images at the site. Ideally, it will be possible to differentiate the neighboring groups that face different directions, but researchers should be prepared to be flexible when defining groups and assigning panel numbers.

FIGURE 2.1. Mark Willis using the rover unit in a global navigation satellite system to get the panel location with an accuracy in centimeters. Photograph by Amanda Castañeda.

At this point, accurate locations for each of the panels should be collected. In much of their research, archaeologists use global positioning instruments for models that are accurate to between 3 to 5 meters. For high-precision mapping of rock art panels, artifacts, and other features, Real Time Kinetics (RTK) is a tool that enhances the precision of position data provided by global navigation satellite systems (GNSS). The RTK system works with two GNSS receivers, one of which is an immobile base station that is set up with a good view of the sky. The base station records variations in incoming signals and then broadcasts corrections to a mobile rover unit. It shows the GNSS rover unit's location in real time and is accurate to within several centimeters.

Panels are identified with pin flags during an initial walk-through of the site, and once all have been found, panel numbers are written on small pieces of blue painter's tape and affixed to the wall at the base of each panel. Features and artifacts frequently associated with rock art panels, such as bedrock metates and mortars, are identified, and their length, width, and depth are recorded. Cultural features such as rock walls, alignments, cairns, hearths, and middens are flagged and later included on the site map. Time-sensitive artifacts such as projectile points and ceramics are also described.

Site recorders must be very careful to search the ground beneath the panels for rock fragments with adhering paint or incised lines indicating that the pieces were once part of a nearby pictograph or petroglyph image. These small remnants frequently became detached when the original figure was painted or inscribed on the types of rock that fracture easily, such as some rhyolites and limestones. The tools used in the manufacture of rock art are also frequently found near the panels they were used to create. Fist-sized chunks of a hard stone like quartzite often occur close to pecked petroglyphs. One end will have been worked to a point on the side opposite where it fits in the hand, and invariably the point would have become battered following continuous striking of the rock wall.

At the base of incised petroglyphs, the most commonly recovered tools are thin flakes from chert or another highly silicified rock type. They are about the size of a guitar pick and have smoothed edges from their use in incising the design. Even if these flaked tools are larger,

FIGURE 2.2. A paint palette at a site in southern New Mexico. The palette, which was face down when first discovered, was next to a bedrock metate. Photograph by Lawrence Loendorf.

they will still have smoothed edges that indicate how they were used. Pieces of sandstone that have one or more smoothed sides are another kind of tool found beneath either abraded petroglyphs, or petroglyphs that were created on top of a smoothed or abraded surface.

In addition to the most commonly found tools used to manufacture petroglyphs, variations in tool design and material have occurred in association with atypical petroglyphs. At a site in the Sacramento Mountains of New Mexico, SSR recorded a petroglyph site with very fine stipple-pecked images. And in a small crevice in the rock face was an elongated, water-washed pebble, battered on both ends, that had been left there after being used. It was apparently handheld, but it may also have acted as a punch after being placed on the rock and hit by a second stone used as a hammer. Very little is known about the size and shape of the punches that were used to create more-refined pecking.

FIGURE 2.3. The small hole in the rock surface where a pecking tool was stored at a site in southern New Mexico. Photograph by Mark Willis.

FIGURE 2.4. This pecking tool's battered ends show that it was used in making the stipple-pecked petroglyphs at the site. Photograph by Mark Willis.

Tools used to make rock paintings have also been found near pictograph panels. Yucca brushes with frayed ends still coated with paint were lying at the base of walls covered with painted hands in dry caves in Canyon de Chelly. Cancellous fragments of bones used to apply paint have been recovered in excavations below paintings, notably in the excavation of Pictograph Cave near Billings, Montana. These samples were radiocarbon dated to between AD 1480 and 1620 (Scott et al. 2014), which is consistent with the estimated age of some of the paintings in the cave. Pieces of bone with adhering paint were found in an excavation at Valley of the Shields in the Pryor Mountains of Montana (Loendorf and Scott-Cummings 2016) and may represent the bone applicators known to have been used by Plains tribes in painting hides. They might also be the remnants of bone ingredients in the paint mixture. In either case, their presence emphasizes the importance of looking for paint-bearing bone fragments as part of an examination of the sediments at the base of a painted wall.

The tools used to grind pigments and mix paint are almost as frequently found as paint applicators. Small, flat rocks with metate-like depressions on the underside have often been used to process pigments, but unless they are inverted, stains from the process can go undetected. Sometimes a natural indentation in a rock was used to hold liquid paint, but if the rock has no other modification, these receptacles are only recognizable if there is paint staining the rock.

Many smaller natural features of a rock surface may have been incorporated into a rock art design. At a site in New Mexico, for example, a petroglyph of a horned serpent was situated below and oriented toward a red sun-like circle formed by an iron concretion. The sun symbol and horned serpent are often associated and form a common pair in Pueblo ethnography that, in this instance, is translated into visual form (Loendorf, Miller, Kemp, White, and Willis 2013:21–40; Schaafsma 2000:118–119).

Natural cracks in a panel surface have also been incorporated into rock art designs, particularly to indicate emergence. The image of a bear is often depicted as having partially emerged from its den, its torso visible on the rock wall while its hindquarters are still surfacing through a crack in the rock. In other instances, bear paw petroglyphs extend into a crevice to evoke the same image. Protuberances in rock surfaces have also been incorporated into the design of a figure to represent, for example, the hump of a bison.

As the assignment of panel numbers at a site proceeds, rock art recorders usually notice the sorts of natural surface features that have been incorporated into rock art images. A more detailed evaluation and description of these associated panel features are presented in "Step 5: Relationships with Features of the Surrounding Environment."

STEP 3

Photographic Documentation

The primary tool used to record rock art is the camera, a device whose family tree is centuries long (Loendorf 2001; Loendorf et al. 1998). Generations of offspring have proceeded from the extremely simple camera obscura of the fifteenth century to the increasingly complex digital camera developed in 1988. The camera held in 1928 by Burt Cosgrove (Figure 3.1) resembles the Kodak Autographic Junior 1A Bellows that is still used today by collectors because of its excellent optics. Vintage cameras are nonetheless cumbersome compared to their smaller digital descendants, and the film they use requires multistep chemical processing, which permits some enhancement of the printed image, although modification is limited.

Some might argue that contemporary film cameras are still useful because the archival quality of their black-and-white film produces better long-term preservation. Experience demonstrates, however, that most of the issues involving archival storage of digital photographs are resolved by the quality of the paper on which they are printed. In fact, the long-term survival of color photographs is better in digital formats because color film, no matter how it is stored, tends to deteriorate over time.

The question of which digital camera to use for recording rock art has multiple answers depending on the preference of the photographer. Advocates for cameras produced by Canon, Nikon, Sony, and other manufacturers all assert that their choices work well for photo-

FIGURE 3.1. Burt Cosgrove getting an overhead view of a site feature in the 1930s. Photograph courtesy of Carolyn O'Bagy Davis.

graphing rock art as long as they include interchangeable lenses. To use a flash unit, a remote shutter release, or other attachment, the camera must have a bracket, called a hot shoe, into which accessories and their sensor units fit.

Photographers working on recent Sacred Sites Research (SSR) projects have used Canon 5D EOS medium-format digital cameras with a Canon EF 24–70mm L USM zoom lens. Camera models change, however, so the goal is to find one that works well for rock art photography. Images are usually captured in the unprocessed and uncompressed raw format, after which processing is done in Adobe Lightroom or a similar program that converts files into TIFF or JPEG formats. There are many variations on this darkroom replacement process, and the standard JPEG image is an acceptable format for photographing rock art.

The production of a formal set of photographs of the overall site as well as the individual panels is a requirement of rock art recording. A menu board, or mug board, containing the site number, panel number, and date is placed adjacent to the panel to identify the resulting photograph for the site record.[1] A scale may be attached to the menu board or set separately on the panel. If stability is problematic, a crew member may be asked to hold the mug board in position as the photograph is taken.

It is not unusual to see the menu board from the corner café with its stick-on plastic letters called into service, although on some SSR projects there have been too few correct letters. For example, Site 24CB4444, Panel 4, requires six 4s, but often there are only five 4s in the letter box. Partly for this reason, it is more practical to use a chalkboard or whiteboard to record the information required for an official site photograph. Archaeologists are increasingly using electronic tablets as menu boards.

Federal agencies and state historic preservation offices (SHPOs) often request that a north-pointing arrow be placed in the site's official photographs. While directional information is important in panoramic images of a landscape or site, it contributes confusion

1. There is no single system for numbering sites, although the Smithsonian trinomial system has been used in the United States since the 1930s and remains popular. New Mexico archaeologists, for example, have always used a number beginning with LA, identifying the site as recorded at the Laboratory of Anthropology. Federal land management agencies and military installations have their own systems in which more than one number can be assigned to a site. Individuals working with rock art site recording are advised to learn the local numbering system(s).

FIGURE 3.2. It is standard practice to have a set of overview photographs for each of the site's panels with an identification board such as the one held here by Hopi consultant Joel Nicholas. Photograph by Lawrence Loendorf.

rather than clarity when photographing a north-facing cliff wall: Should the arrow be pointed up or down? Placement of a directional arrow on a south-facing panel presents the same problem. Since the direction faced by a rock art panel is noted in the written report completed for each panel, a north arrow is not needed in panel photographs. If the panel is on a horizontal surface, which infrequently occurs, then a north arrow can contribute important information. In fact, SSR recorders have found petroglyphs of katsina faces on flat bedrock surfaces that are oriented toward the rising sun (Loendorf, Miller, Kemp, White, and Willis 2013). Whether or not a north arrow is included in the photograph, the direction faced by the photographer should be noted in the photo log.

Getting Good Light

When celebrated landscape photographer Ansel Adams (1935) observed that "you don't take a photograph, you make it," he could have been commenting on the relationship between a successful photograph of a rock art image and the quality of the light illuminating it. A practice followed by rock art photographers is to observe

FIGURE 3.3. When a panel is partially shaded, it is often helpful to totally shade the figures while taking photos and drawing panels. Photograph by Lawrence Loendorf.

panels at different times during the day, when the quality and direction of the light are often very different. This is particularly important at a large site. The appearance of a figure—particularly the visibility of its details—is often enhanced by early morning and late afternoon light, while the same figure in shade or full sunlight may look completely different. On large sites, where recording takes place over several days, photographers keep notes on the clarity of the petroglyphs and pictographs produced by various light conditions.

Reflectors are a standard piece of equipment that rock art photographers use to "make" a photograph. Collapsible round or oval reflectors with silver- or gold-colored fabrics, available in camera stores, are used to direct sunlight across a rock art panel, enhancing the effects provided by natural light. Reflectors can also be used to partially or fully shade a panel, creating a more even light. Umbrellas produce a more diffuse light, and their handles make them easier to manipulate.

When photographing rock art, some form of artificial light, usually from a camera's flash attachment, is nearly always used in combination with natural light. This is particularly true in caves or settings where natural light is unavailable. The directional lighting provided by a sidelight flash is widely used to help bring out the texture of a faint petroglyph (Loendorf et al. 1998). In the past, a photographer's dexterity was challenged by dealing with the cords connecting the flash to a camera, but—technology to the rescue—the advent of wireless flash units now makes that connection electronically.

Since the development in the late 1960s of light-emitting diodes (LEDs), the application of this technology has become widespread. Everything from highway signs to flat-panel TVs to smart watches employ LED technology in some form. Battery-operated LED light panels have become another device for photographing rock art in dark settings such as caves or for creating sidelight to reveal fine details in petroglyphs.

DStretch

The images produced by digital cameras can be manipulated by increasingly complex software that rock art researchers have been prompt to exploit. Nearly 30 years ago, Jon Harman, a specialist in medical imaging who also had an interest in recording rock art, adapted the decorrelation stretch algorithm for use in a computer software program, DStretch, to enhance faint painted rock images. Although it is not necessary to grasp the mathematical principles embodied by DStretch's DNA, Harman's website has links to the meaning of the term as well as descriptions of the complex programming underlying the technique.[2] There are comparisons of DStretch with other photographic enhancement programs (e.g., Cerrillo-Cuenca and Sepulveda 2015). In another work, Henderson (2002) discusses the importance of lighting in any enhancement software.

Even as rock art researchers have become aware of the contributions that DStretch can make to the visualization of nearly imperceptible painted images, Harman has continued to tweak the algorithms, selecting the channels that provide the most clarity for different colors of rock art paint.

The results are often stunning. When Hattie Cosgrove sketched Element K at Picture Cave in 1929, the figure was partially visible, but a digital photograph taken in 2011 revealed only a faint suggestion of red paint. Figure 3.4 illustrates the deterioration of the image as well as its restoration in a DStretch enhancement, which shows that the image is an inverted goggle-eye entity.

2. https://dstretch.com.

a

c

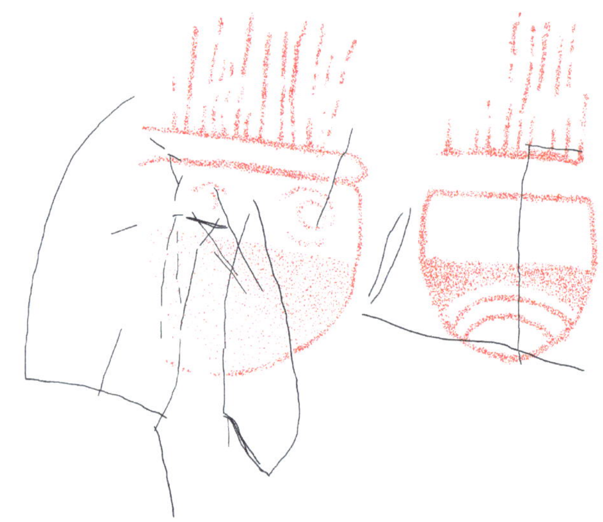

FIGURE 3.4. An example of the effectiveness of DStretch software. Figure 3.4a is an untouched photograph that shows mainly scratched graffiti on the rock surface, but in DStretch (Figure 3.4b) two red katsina faces, or masks, are visible. Figure 3.4c is a photo tracing of the faces/masks with graffiti. Figure 3.4d shows the two faces/masks without the graffiti. Photograph by Lawrence Loendorf; line drawing by Laurie White.

b

d

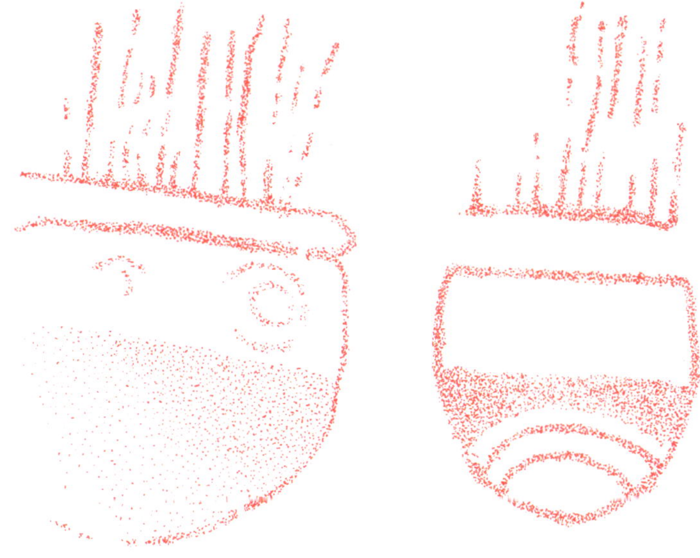

The DStretch software is available for purchase to use with a camera phone or a tablet, but it requires the prior installation of Image J, for which it is a plug-in. Image J, a Java-based image processing program, was originally developed at the National Institutes of Health and the Laboratory for Optical and Computational Instrumentation. It is in the public domain and available at the National Institutes of Health website.[3] DStretch can be downloaded directly from the DStretch website. Once it is installed on a computer, a digital photograph can be opened using Image J. Detailed instructions for manipulating the process of image enhancement—using color spaces accessible by choosing channels like RGB, YDS, and others—are available on the website. An advantage for rock art research is that a cell phone can take photos of known or suspected pictographs that can later be checked in DStretch to see if they are visible. In addition to helping with reconnaissance, these images are often helpful to artists who are creating scale drawings of the rock art panels.

New and innovative techniques for recording rock art continue to be developed. Recently retroReveal, a software hosted by the University of Utah's J. Willard Marriott Library, has been successfully used to enhance faded rock art images. The software exposes details not seen by DStretch, and individuals who have used it recommend using both retroReveal and DStretch to capture faded details (Andrews and Brink 2022; Minick and Keyser 2022). Unfortunately, the software is currently no longer available for public use, but other photo enhancement programs, such as Adobe Photoshop, can also be effective in bringing out rock art details.

Pole Photography

Many rock art panels are in inaccessible places, even beyond the reach of researchers using ladders or scaffolds. Mounting a digital camera on a pole to record a rock art panel high on a canyon wall is a relatively simple solution and requires only three pieces of equipment. The first is a collapsible pole, available at most hardware stores. A sturdy one that comes in several lengths has the trade name Mr. LongArm. An adapter attached at one end to the camera and to the pole at the other completes this useful tool.

3. https://imagej.nih.gov/ij/download.html.

FIGURE 3.5. A team of researchers using pole photography to record a high rock art panel. Mark Willis is holding the pole with the camera; Laurie White has another with the flash unit; and Lawrence Loendorf is using the remote to simultaneously trigger the flash and camera shutter. Photograph by Maya Bontrager.

The final piece of equipment for pole photography is a two-part wireless remote shutter release, one part of which attaches to the hot shoe on the camera, while the other is used to operate the shutter from a distance. Not all remote shutter releases are compatible with all camera models, so it is important to read the specifications before purchasing one.

For best results, pole photography is a two-person process, requiring one person to hold the camera pole and the other to press the remote shutter release. If only one person is available, the process requires considerable strength and dexterity. The weight of many SLR digital cameras requires the recorder to use one hand to stabilize the pole, which is often extended to 12 feet, while operating the shutter with the other hand.

Mounting a flash on a second pole is a useful variation of pole photography developed by Mark Willis. The flash can be aimed toward the top, bottom, sides, and all points in between of a petroglyph as directed by the operator of the pole-mounted camera. A model of the petroglyph is then created by using software to overlap all of the images from the different angles. This technique uses some of the principles of reflective transformation imaging and allows petroglyphs with exceptionally fine lines, even 2 meters above the ground, to be photographed. The drawback, however, is that three people are required. If the recorder is working alone, and the panel is not too high, using a selfie stick is an inexpensive way to photograph rock art.

GigaPan Photography

In 2004, researchers began adapting GigaPan photo technology, developed by NASA for the Mars rovers Spirit and Opportunity, for use in widely different applications. The term—which is a combination of the word segments "giga" (a number so large that it is written as 10^9) and "pan" (the initial syllable of "panoramic")—refers to high-resolution panoramic photographs of scenes as diverse as vast Martian landscapes, the thousands of people attending President Obama's inauguration, huge crowds assembled for sporting events, and expansive rock art sites. What began as a solution to the scientific problem of producing a high-definition panoramic image has enabled Facebook subscribers to zoom into a GigaPan image stored online, find and tag themselves, and share the result across social media.

A combination of hardware—a digital camera and an automatic tripod—and photo-processing software can be made to produce one large image by integrating hundreds of smaller photos. GigaPan technology can not only capture the full width of a rock art panel, but also permits a close-up focus on a panel's details. Rock art researchers Robert Mark and Evelyn Billo (2011) have reported on the techniques and equipment they used in creating GigaPan images at sites in Texas and Arizona. In 2010, on the other side of the world, members of the Arabian Rock Art Research Project started using GigaPan equipment and software to record several petroglyph sites in remote desert settings in Saudi Arabia. To demonstrate the utility of the process, they have made a selection of photographs available online for viewers to manipulate. By moving a mouse or using a touchpad, a large-scale photo can be enlarged to show tiny details—for example, the individual dromedaries carved into a sandstone outcrop.[4] A drawback to a GigaPan image, however, is that it cannot be printed but must be viewed and studied using a computer.

Structure from Motion (SfM)

Structure from Motion (SfM) is another new digital technology advancing the ability of researchers to record rock art more completely and accurately. Using SfM, a 3D model of a rock art surface (the structure) can be created by taking multiple overlapping 2D photographs from many different angles using a digital camera (the motion). Photo-processing software in the camera then matches common points in the individual photographs and knits them together into a 3D image that is so exact it can be used to measure the image it replicates.

Mark Willis and SSR now use SfM to record 3D models for all significant panels found during a recording project. Because this technique is camera-based, it is much less expensive and less complicated to collect data in the field than it is with laser scanning equipment. Anywhere a camera can be carried, 3D data can be generated. (For examples of archaeological applications of SfM technology see Brown et al. 2010; Kenmotsu et al. 2012; Liebman et al. 2013; and Willis and Jalandoni 2011.)

4. https://saudi-archaeology.com/gigapan/.

SfM is one example of the application of sophisticated recording techniques to the recording and visualization of rock art images in their physical setting. Further processing capabilities may be heading in the direction of 4D enhancement of photographic data that would document changes to a rock art panel over time. Such a technology would enable future researchers to observe, document, and, ideally, intervene in the destruction of fragile rock art resources.

STEP 4

Panel Forms, Measured Drawings, and Tracings

Although photography is an essential component of the process of recording a rock art panel and its individual figures, a static photo must be augmented by important information that a recorder can include in a drawing, and a researcher can observe and manually record on a document designed for that purpose. Since some land-managing agencies stipulate the use of specific panel recording forms, awareness of the sponsoring agency's requirements is a prerequisite to producing an acceptable panel form.

Some basic terminology is used during this step in the rock art recording process. Archaeologists refer to the individual figures that make up the overall panel as elements. A row of 10 short, vertical lines oriented parallel to one another, for example, would be identified as a row of counter lines and classified as one element instead of 10. There would then be a note in the accompanying site report that such an element consists of more than one motif—a motif being a figure or design that occurs with enough frequency to become recognizable. The term "element" is nearly always assigned to a single motif on a panel, but there are instances in which several closely related motifs are designated as one element.

Archaeologists who record rock art often disagree about the descriptive names they apply to the elements they identify. Some recorders avoid species-specific terms such as "bison," for example, because it excludes a perhaps more accurate identification of the figure. Similarly, if a recorder notes that a figure "looks like a bird," it is thereafter seen as a bird when, in fact, it may be a wavy line.

Partly for this reason, more general terms like "quadruped" and "zoomorph" are often used to describe motifs that have four legs or look like snakes or birds. On the other hand, sometimes it is useful for the recorder to make a judgment about the species of a figure designated as an element. When a figure looks like a dragonfly, for example, it can be helpful to identify it as "dragonfly-like." Plant forms are often described in a similar way. While it might be possible to distinguish and identify a corn plant, other plants are not as distinctive. Sometimes the neologism "veggie-morph" has been used to describe an element, even though the term "plant-like" is sufficient.

Basic Panel Data

The information collected about a rock art panel can vary from one researcher to another, but every researcher begins by noting the same basic data. Initial observations include the type of rock and the manufacturing technique used to make the images, as well as the height and width of the panel and the direction it faces. The panel's number and its relationship to neighboring panels may be apparent on a good site map, but it is still important to record that, for instance, the panel is the most westerly at the site, or that it is high on the cliff face, 2 meters to the right of another numbered panel. Noting how far the lowest and highest elements are above the current ground surface, or whether portions of the panel are buried, can help establish the panel's age. Information about the panel's condition and whether it has been compromised by graffiti or bullet holes is important to include. Short descriptions of the elements on the panel are also essential.

If the site owner or land-managing agency does not have a preferred panel form, it is permissible for a recorder to design one that includes basic data determined by personal preference. Appendix A includes a comprehensive panel form, and step-by-step instructions for its completion are in Appendix B.

Measured Drawings

In the process of making a measured drawing, a researcher creates another version of the rock art being recorded. The lens involved is the human eye, and the hand and arm mimic the action of the bones and muscles of the image's original creator. The intimacy involved, particularly in the production of a drawing or tracing, is such that more detail is often captured by this technique than appears in a photograph.

Measured drawings are done to scale and are the equivalent of plan-view drawings in standard archaeological research. One of their important functions is to identify elements within a panel, typically using a sequence of lowercase letters (beginning with *a, b, c*) so that descriptions and measurements noted on the panel form are linked to the appropriate figures. Another technique for designating elements is to put gridlines on the sides of the panel drawing, with sequential numbers (*1, 2, 3*) placed on the horizontal axis and consecutive uppercase letters (*A, B, C*) arranged vertically on one side. Individual figures or elements can then be described as being within a section, such as 2B.

Panel drawings are also used to identify instances of superposition and other panel details. Because individuals completing panel drawings see considerably more detail than photographers do, especially with the correct light, a panel drawing is the only way that finely incised or scratched figures can be recorded. Portions of such petroglyphs may be visible in a photograph, but a complete recording requires that they be traced or drawn in the field, where the accuracy of the drawn image can be checked and rechecked.

The working conditions that panel recorders must prepare for include rocky surfaces, pack rat nests, cactus spines, and loose, slippery sediments, which means that various kinds of gear must be brought to the field. A three-legged folding stool provides stability for a person sitting in front of a panel, and a kneeling pad or knee pads provide protection when figures at the base of a panel are recorded. The bulky crash pads used by rock climbers enable supine artists to record images on the ceiling of a rockshelter, but carrying them to a remote site along with all the other equipment requires endurance. A folded piece of canvas can be unfolded and used as a ground cover, with what it lacks in comfort being made up for by its ease of transport.

The recording artist's backpack will contain tools and supplies for making measured drawings. Metric folding rules are essential and are available in wood and fiberglass at many hardware stores. Wooden ones, which are more durable, are widely available. Most recorders

FIGURE 4.1. Sara Scott and Susan Hovde using a metric folding rule to put a tape grid on the panel. The grid is very helpful to the artist drawing a field sketch of the panel. Photograph by Amanda Castañeda.

use storage clipboards to hold the pencils, erasers, and metric graph paper needed for their drawings, although some prefer larger boards that have clips on several sides.

The initial step in preparing to make a panel drawing is to open the metric folding rule so that it forms an L-shape. The vertical and horizontal segments will be used to measure the height and width of the panel, respectively, either by attaching the rule to the rock surface with tape or by using it to indicate where small pieces of tape, never left overnight, should be attached at 10-centimeter or 20-centimeter intervals to create grid squares. Even though painter's tape contains very little adhesive and isn't harmful to the rock surface, care must be taken to avoid contact with the rock art images and unstable rock surfaces. The artist will be aware of any grid points that have been omitted and will add them mentally when creating the field drawing.

Using tape may not be allowed at some sites, so permission may be required prior to labeling panels with tape or using it in grid marks. An agreement between the site recorders and the site's owners or

FIGURE 4.2. Mark Willis using a panel of LED lights to illuminate a panel of incised lines in a cave. Photograph by Gilles Tosello.

FIGURE 4.3. Mary Hopkins and Laurie White using a reflector to study a panel of incised petroglyphs. Photograph by Amanda Castañeda.

managers regarding site recording procedures must be made clear prior to beginning the project.

The collapsible reflectors used to direct light toward a panel being photographed are equally useful in the drawing and tracing processes. For some close work, a mirror can help reveal incised lines by directing sunlight across a surface. LED lights work well in caves where little light is available.

Because the field drawing will be reworked later in the laboratory, the goal of the rock art recording artist is to complete a basic sketch in the field. Rock features such as cracks or eroded areas are usually sketched first, followed by anything adhering to the surface, such as lichens. Once the naturally occurring properties of the background have been sketched, the motifs themselves are added.

Tracing Rock Art Panels

The development and use of tools by the human species is often characterized as the replacement of simple techniques and designs by more complex technologies and materials. The field of rock art recording is an exception to the simple-to-complex trajectory in that both a vintage recording technique like direct field tracing coexists with the more technologically advanced process in which digital tracing is performed using a computer tablet.

Direct field tracing is not without its critics, who argue that placing a transparent, flexible overlay on a panel and tracing the underlying rock art images can have a destructive effect on the figures that the act of recording is designed to protect. Tracing, however, produces a one-to-one replica of the image created by the original artist, and for that reason it continues to be used worldwide. If it is done properly, we believe the technique can produce valuable results, and for this reason it is included in this 10-step approach, although with certain caveats (Greer et al. 2006).

First of all, tracing should only be undertaken by a person who has been trained in the technique by an experienced professional rock art recorder. Equally important is the fact that if the site is on either federal or privately owned land, there may be rules that prohibit any direct field tracing of rock art panels.

Prior to any tracing, the panel surface should be closely inspected to ensure that it is stable and the rock wall is sufficiently consolidated.

FIGURE 4.4. Laurie White and a large panel tracing at the Castle Garden site, Wyoming. Note the use of weighted tripods to help hold the tracing in place. Photograph by Greg White.

Rock surfaces that are exfoliating or that appear likely to fracture are not good candidates for tracing. As a general rule, it is safer to trace panels of petroglyphs rather than pictographs, particularly if lumps of pigment were used to create the paintings, or if the pigment was mixed with tallow to form a crayon-like applicator. Some pigment tends to remain on the surface of rock paintings that were made with crayons, and even the light pressure associated with tracing can cause it to rub off. Pictographs made with liquid paint are more stable and better candidates for tracing. If there is any doubt about the stability of a rock surface or painted image, *do not trace*. Instead, make a measured drawing and use it along with photographs to create a digital tracing.

Direct field tracings are made by placing a sheet of clear acetate film over the rock art panel. Acetate film is available in varying thicknesses and can be purchased in rolls from which pieces of the required length can be cut. The film is held in place by attaching pieces of low-adhesive tape to the rock surface around the edges of the acetate. Different colors of Sharpie pens are used to trace different components of the panel: for example, petroglyphs are drawn in black, lichens are outlined in green, and cracks in the rock are marked in brown.

SSR worked with the Bureau of Land Management on a major project to trace the Castle Gardens rock art site in central Wyoming, during which we developed techniques that allowed us to minimize the amount of tape used (Loendorf et al. 2012). Tripods or photography light stands were leaned against the tracing plastic and weighted with plastic bags filled with rocks. A tennis ball pushed onto the top of the tripod allows it to twist into the rock surface for a good bond.

Computer-Assisted Tracing

None of the paraphernalia required to trace a panel of rock art images by hand is involved in the initial step of computer tracing. A digital camera replaces the acetate film, tape, and Sharpie pens that a recorder uses in the field to create an accurate representation of one or more figures. Instead, multiple high-resolution photographs are taken of the panels using RAW format and then imported into a tablet computer, where software programs such as Adobe Photoshop digitally rectify the images. Field drawings and tracings can also be scanned or photographed, or hung against a white backdrop and illuminated prior to photographing, uploading, and processing. At this point, experienced recorders can use a stylus to trace directly onto a computer screen, or they can work on a Wacom digital drawing tablet or similar hardware.

The tracing software creates individual layers for specific features of the panels: for example, one layer depicting the cracks in the rock surface, another layer devoted to surface vegetation such as lichens, one with the rock art images, and additional layers for any other features that have been identified. As tracing progresses, photographs of the panel are constantly revisited to ensure that accuracy is maintained, and a final trip to the site may take place at the conclusion of the process to compare tracings to the original rock art images. After a drawing is finished, it is saved as both a high-resolution layered TIFF file and a JPEG file, which can be printed on 8½ × 11-inch paper and inserted into the final report along with the survey forms.

Since both direct field tracing and computer tracing can produce accurate replicas of rock art imagery, it is likely that both techniques will continue to be used in decades to come.

STEP 5

Relationships with Features of the Surrounding Environment

The research involved in Step 5 begins when the site is first discovered and continues as the photographers and artists work, learning its nuances and distinctive nature. It is the equivalent of a continuous quality control review to ensure that every feature of the site and its setting has been recorded. Because it is easy to become focused exclusively on the rock images, a short checklist of other features to note would include mimetoliths, medicinal plants, power animal homes and caves, the viewshed, archaeoastronomy, acoustics, and shrines.

Mimetoliths

Rocks and rocky outcrops containing natural formations that resemble humans or animals are called mimetoliths. Eroded rocks often appear to be mimetoliths, and cracks and cave openings may also contribute to the definition of a figure. Mimetoliths may be large, in which case an animal or human figure is represented by an entire outcrop, or they can be a smaller part of a rock surface, such as two holes, side by side, which are incorporated as eyes in a face. These features have been created by wind or other weathering agents without human interaction, although there are instances in which a part of the feature has been augmented to improve its resemblance to an animal or body part.

Sometimes a change of focus or perspective is required to see a mimetolith, and in some ways it is a learned skill requiring that an open mind override a skeptical attitude. Native Americans who work on rock art projects, many of whom have extensive experience in

FIGURE 5.1. Cascadia Cave, Oregon. This mimetolith, a fish-shaped rockshelter, is dominated by images of bear paws. Photograph by Lawrence Loendorf.

natural settings and outdoor activities, are often the first to notice a mimetolith. Another advantage is that they are often participants in a cultural tradition in which their elders have referred to rock outcrops with animal names. Knowledge of the Native American tradition of assigning place-names has increased significantly following Keith Basso's (1996) pioneering research on the Western Apache.

Any discussion of archaeology and landscapes must recognize the association of mimetoliths with rock art. An excellent example occurs in the Cascadia Cave site in Oregon, a rockshelter in soft volcanic tuff that measures 14 meters long by 6 meters high, and 5 meters to 7 meters from the dripline to the back of the shelter (Poetschat et al. 2010). More than 50 bear paw petroglyphs occur in the shelter along with images of horizontal wavy lines, other abstract forms, and a few simple human faces. The cave opening itself is shaped like a salmon, and there is a crack in the back wall in the anatomical location where a gill would occur. This fish-shaped mimetolith went unnoticed by the dozens of archaeologists who worked at the site until a nine-year-old

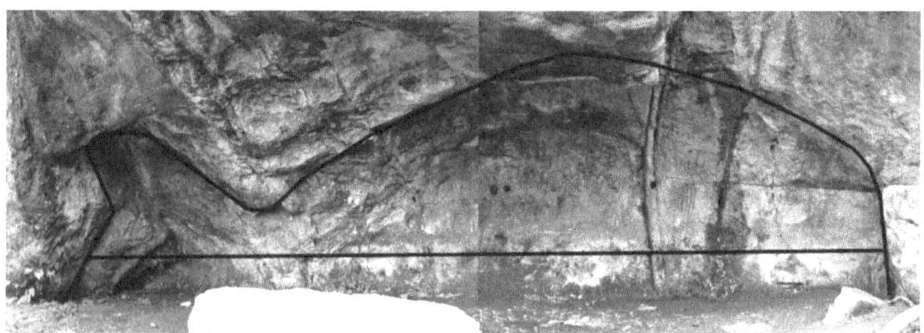

FIGURE 5.2. Schematic showing the fish-shaped outline of Cascadia Cave, Oregon. Illustration courtesy of David Kaiser.

girl visiting on a field trip asked the guide about the opening whose shape looked to her like a fish swimming upstream in the direction of salmon spawning in the nearby river (Poetschat et al. 2010:66).

Once the fish shape was recognized, it was clear that the presence of bear paw images referred to the fact that in the late summer and fall, bears in the Pacific Northwest catch salmon. Native groups in Washington and Oregon have First Salmon ceremonies presided over by a shaman known as the Salmon Chief, whose spirit assistant is a bear. It is suggested that folklore about a salmon that turned into stone might refer to the Cascadia Cave mimetolith (Poetschat et al. 2010:67), but the broader conclusion to be drawn from this example is that the outline of the rock feature is the key to understanding the meaning of the petroglyph features associated with it.

Medicinal Plants

Careful examination of the varieties of plants at a site should occur concurrently with other Step 5 tasks. The purpose of such scrutiny is not to identify surrounding vegetation but to focus on the plants growing at the base of the rock art panels. Especially in the Southwest, medicinal or psychotropic species such as *Nicotiana attentuata* and other tobacco variants are often found growing near rock art panels (Loendorf et al. 2015). It is unclear whether tobacco was consumed at the site, left as an offering, or both, but the association of rock art and tobacco is strong in southern New Mexico, Arizona, Nevada, and Utah (Winter 2000). Tobacco may also be present at rock art sites in other locations but has gone unnoticed by recording archaeologists.

FIGURE 5.3. A wild tobacco plant growing at the base of a pictograph site in southern New Mexico. Photograph by Lawrence Loendorf.

Datura (*Datura* spp.) is another plant that is commonly present at rock art sites in southern latitudes. Its geographical distribution is limited by the temperatures in colder climates, but other plants in the Solanaceae family are hardier and can occur at rock art sites in a wide range of ecosystems. Texas Mountain Laurel (*Sophora secundiflora*), also known as the Mescal Bean plant, is often found in proximity to southern rock art sites. Sometimes partially chewed lumps of plant material, called quids, are recovered at rock art sites; examples include the Datura quids that were tucked into crevices in a California cave (Robinson et al. 2020) and the red mescal beans found at sites in southern New Mexico (Miller et al. 2019).

Power Animal Homes and Dens

Animals whose spiritual energy is believed to inhabit places and special people such as shamans are referred to as power animals. Their presence is suggested by the association of dens typical of their species and the representation of these animals in rock art panels. Rattlesnakes use the same dens for hundreds, if not thousands, of years, and it is common to find rock art depictions of snakes near these long-term dens. Similarly, eagle nests are often found where images of eagles or thunderbirds occur on nearby rock formations. Images of bears and bear paws are frequently placed in crevices or adjacent to holes in the rock, suggesting that these animals are emerging from their dens.

During the recording of rock art at Picture Cave in Texas, SSR crew members noticed that every 10 minutes or so, a small bird flew into the deeper recesses of the cave. Identified as a Rock Wren (*Salpinctes obsoletus*), it is a member of the Troglodytidae family, whose dietary habits include searching for insects in caves (Miller et al. 2012). In doing so, it was believed, the Rock Wrens served ancient Puebloans as messengers to the clouds or to the mountaintops enclosed in clouds where katsinas, the ancestral spirits of the people, lived. The small birds were therefore the connection between the underworld and the sky world.

Viewshed

Although the primary focus when recording rock art is on the site and its panels, an important perspective is provided by remembering to look out at what the site and its figures are "seeing" in the landscape: the viewshed. This approach is part of a much larger field of inquiry known as viewshed archaeology, which acknowledges that the view of the prominent mountain in the distance may be an important reason for the placement and subjects of a rock art panel. In some instances, the view from a rock art site might include sacred mountains or another rock art locality, suggesting that the two sites are connected by spirit trails.

Archeoastronomy

Sky watchers in the past used variations in the tempo and movement of sunlight and shadow across earthly features as a means of ordering their world. Archeoastronomy is a complicated subject with its own research goals that extend beyond the scope of this book, but when recording a rock art site, it is important to note the relationship between the site and important celestial processes such as the rising and setting of the sun, and any solstice or equinox phenomena.

A site report normally includes data on the direction each panel faces, which means that the site's orientation to the sun is noted. Usually, however, a sun/shadow relationship with the images would be made obvious by the presence of a gnomon, or notch, in the rock itself through which the sun would focus as it rises. In the American Southwest, figures such as spirals are more likely to be associated with calendrical events (McHugh et al. 2021; Schaeffer and Stamm 2020), and bison are closely associated with the sun in Great Plains settings (Albers 2003; Loendorf and Conner 2020). Any motifs that are known to be associated with the sun should receive extra attention during this phase of the recording effort.

Acoustics

The study of the sounds associated with rock art sites, sometimes called archaeoacoustics, is a relatively new field, but efforts to understand the sonic conditions that may have influenced the selection of a site by ancient people are increasingly common. The acoustical associations with rock art occur on three general levels: one, echoes that reverberate from the rock art panels; two, sites that amplify sound in such a way that it carries to other parts of the site or beyond; and three, the presence of "ringing rocks," rock features that produce musical tones when struck.

Since the 1980s, archaeologist Steven Waller (1993) has been carrying a spring-loaded trap to rock art sites and recording the echo resulting from release of the snapping arm. His goal is to find sites with echoes that suggest the images are talking to the viewer, and his pioneering research has produced significant discoveries. Waller and others use a variety of noise-producing implements in their investigations, including a starter pistol, but simply clapping hands when recording a site is an effective way to discover if echoes can be produced.

Sites that amplify sound are usually in settings that have a conch-shell shape that makes it possible to hear voices from a distance. At one site in southern New Mexico, it is possible to hear the voices of people speaking at a normal level nearly half a kilometer away (Miller et al. 2019:260). Given the appropriate site structure, playing a flute or some other instrument in a cave would have reverberated across the landscape.

"Ringing rocks," "lithophones," "rock gongs," and "bell rocks" are terms used to refer to rock formations in southeast Asia, Africa, and elsewhere in the world that produce musical sounds and are often associated with rock art. The Gobustan petroglyphs in Baku, Azerbaijan, and the musical rocks making up the formations there are so abundant that they have been placed on UNESCO's World Heritage List. The battered or smoothed surfaces of bell rocks are evidence that they have been struck multiple times (Hernbrode and Boyle 2016). Revarnishing can occur, making it more difficult to detect that a rock has been hit repeatedly, but some evidence will remain.

Shrines

Lastly, we should not overlook the rock shrines and fasting beds that are found near rock art sites. These have been mentioned in other sections of this book, but a renewed effort needs to be made to find these features during the closer examination of a panel's surroundings. Shrines are often simple arrangements of just a few stones set together near the site and are referred to by some Native American consultants as prayer stations.

Rock structures that were used as fasting beds are found at sites on the Northern Plains and can be directly associated with panels of

FIGURE 5.4. This small cairn, about 30 meters from a major petroglyph site on land owned by the Gila River Indian Community in Arizona, was identified as a prayer station by an O'odham consultant. Photograph by Lawrence Loendorf.

petroglyphs. Some of these fasting beds are thought to have been left at rock art sites by Apaches and are important examples of the kind of features that researchers should look for (Loendorf 2008:175–178).

STEP 6

Site Mapping

Standard practice in any archaeological investigation is making a preliminary site map, and similarly, during the initial archaeological survey of a rock art site, a sketch map is usually produced. Using a compass and estimating the distances by pacing, a team plots the location of the rock art along with any other site features such as shrines, bedrock mortars, hearths, middens, and rock walls. Artifact clusters, indicating the range of activities that occurred at the site in addition to the painting or excising of the rock surface, are also noted. Taken together, the archaeological remains are often clues to the contexts in which the panels were integrated into a sacred landscape.

First, a datum is placed in a conspicuous location on the edge of the site and then used as the point from which all distances between items and features are measured. It is usually indicated by an 18-inch-long rebar stake to which a tag identifying the site number is attached. Traditionally, the GPS location of the datum has been essential information since it establishes the spatial framework of the site. Contemporary recording of site location data is so accurate, however, that not all land-managing agencies require a site datum. The trend to no longer require a datum necessitates that the recording requirements governing a site be established before recording begins.

Making a map of a site that is being fully recorded is usually done with unmanned aerial vehicles (UAVs), more commonly known as drones. Drones are available from big-box stores for several hun-

FIGURE 6.1. View through the control unit for an unmanned aerial vehicle, or drone. The operator can direct the camera mounted on the drone to photograph ground features or paintings on a cliff wall. Photograph by Mark Willis.

dred dollars and can be fitted with one or more digital cameras to produce the large-scale perspective as well as the fine-grained detail that a complete site map requires. Camera-bearing drones can take photographs in places that might be inaccessible or too dangerous to photograph using other techniques. Other types of drone-mounted cameras can be used for site exploration. For instance, thermal imaging cameras have infrared and near-red capabilities that can identify partially buried features such as stone shrines.

A significant advance in UAV aerial mapmaking has resulted from the mounting of lidar cameras on drones. Lidar (an acronym for “laser imaging, detection, and ranging”) is a technology that archaeologists are using to survey densely covered landscapes, revealing and enabling the mapping of hidden buildings and other structures. Until recently, lidar photography required dozens of flights over an area to produce results and was therefore prohibitively expensive. UAVs are cheaper to operate and have made lidar mapping cost-effective,

FIGURE 6.2. A blimp balloon with a mount for a camera. This technique is useful at sites where the use of drones is prohibited. Photograph by Mark Willis.

although the application of this technology to the mapping of rock art sites, so many of which consist of vertical panels, has yet to be determined.

The increasing use of drones to map cultural sites, by proficient as well as inexperienced researchers, is becoming a serious issue. Regulations governing where and under what circumstances drones can be used apply particularly to areas where air traffic is prevalent. Permits, without which drone use may be totally forbidden, are required in areas such as military bases or national parks. However, aerial photographs of rock art sites can still be taken in some of these locations. Mark Willis has used a camera mounted on a box kite to photograph aerial views, and a blimp balloon can also be mounted with a camera.

If the goal is to create a contour map, digital terrain models provide the elevation of an area of the site's surface, thereby creating contours that capture the elevation of features within the area of the map. The UAV operator should be aware that aerial survey data must be referenced to ground control points. Experience is also required in the placement of ground targets where the horizontal and vertical

FIGURE 6.3. A drone photograph taken by Mark Willis of the canyon wall at the Hole in the Wall site in Wyoming. The panel locations were added later. Photograph by Mark Willis and Amanda Castañeda.

coordinates of the control points can be obtained (referred to as *x* for easting, *y* for northing, and *z* for elevation).

Panel locations can also be recorded using GPS units and then plotted on a contour map. Alternatively, site maps may consist of a photograph that includes both the rock wall face on which the panels have been plotted and the adjacent ground surface. These maps present a view of the actual site setting, which makes them more useful to some viewers.

Aerial views of sites showing panel locations work well for anyone trying to understand the relationships between panels. Often, however, this kind of map will not work for a full site record, which needs to identify site boundaries. United States Geological Survey (USGS) maps provide a good background for plotting the panels, associated features, and a boundary line around them.

The decision to use drones for mapping rock art should be guided by several considerations, foremost among them being weather conditions. High winds make it impossible to control drones, and snow cover or heavy clouds can cast shadows on the ground. Nonetheless,

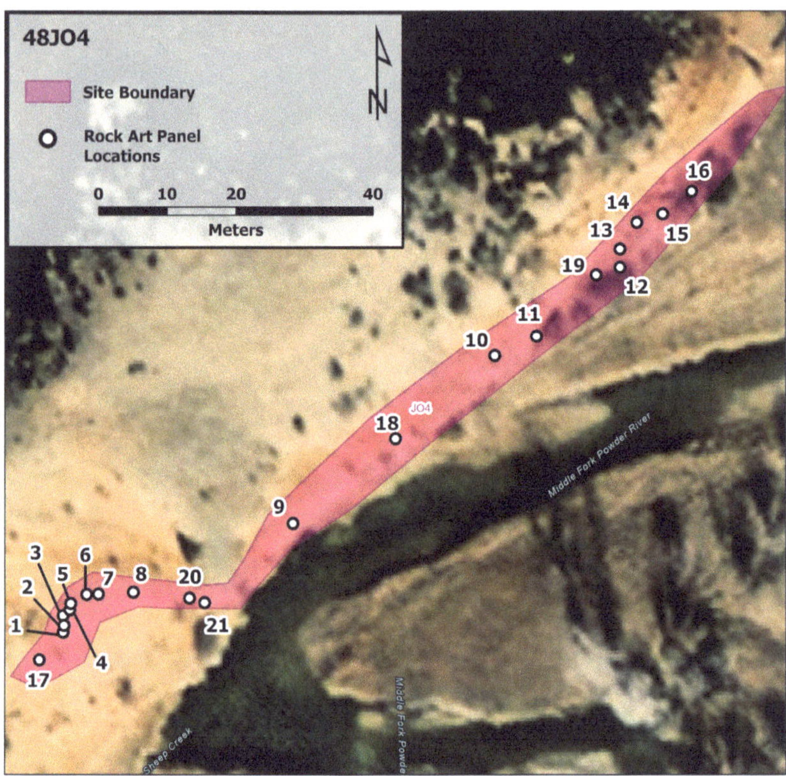

FIGURE 6.4. A site map with boundaries and panel locations. Map by Amanda Castañeda.

an experienced drone operator can often work around these issues by visiting the site early in the day, when the light is good, or by consulting a weather app to determine when wind speeds are conducive to drone use. Of foremost importance is an awareness that the rock art can be damaged if something goes wrong, and that flying a drone close to a panel without sufficient piloting skills is reckless and should not be attempted. Because of the potential for damaging rock art, unlicensed drone use is often forbidden on public lands in much of the world.

Rock art panels that are within a rockshelter or a cave, however, are beyond the range of drones, and mapping them must be done with a compass and tape measure. If the site has a datum, it is important to place it on the map along with the panel locations. Increasingly, archaeologists use laser measuring devices for determining such distance information. The site boundaries often consist of the walls of the rockshelter or cave, whose floors are usually relatively flat, allowing the included contour lines to show the direction in which the floor slopes. If the site boundaries extend outside the cave, then placing contours on a compass-and-tape map is more difficult. They can be extrapolated from a USGS quadrangle map or another contour map.

All maps need to include a north arrow and a scale showing the relationship between the distances indicated on the map and the corresponding actual distances. Maps should also have legends, or keys, that include important details such as the meaning of all symbols, the date the map was made, and the name of the mapmaker.

STEP 7

Compositional Analysis of Pigments

A viewer's initial reaction upon seeing a colorful pictograph, or rock painting, is usually to focus on the image's aesthetic and stylistic properties, such as its design and placement on a rock surface, whether it is part of an arrangement of other similar images or is isolated, and whether it is unique. There is often interest in a pictograph's historical and cultural context if temporal placement can be determined. Once these details have been noted, a rock art researcher's attention usually turns to the properties of the paint used to produce the image: What is it made of, and what makes it adhere to the rock surface? Over the past 30 years, refinements of techniques for geochemical analysis have resulted in a process that is used in a variety of in-field settings and has been adopted by archaeologists to answer those two questions.

Compositional analysis of pictographs is accomplished with the use of portable X-ray fluorescence (pXRF) instruments that most federal agencies, universities, and cultural resource organizations now make available to researchers in many disciplines. An explanation of the principles involved in pXRF analysis would involve a deep dive into the behavior of the atoms in a material such as paint when exposed to ionization, but, fortunately, pXRF is a technology that a researcher can use without acquiring a PhD in physics. Some analytical processes are problematic because they require removing a sample of the material of interest, but pXRF testing is nondestructive and has no negative effect on the rock art painting being analyzed (Newman and Loendorf 2005).

Making Paint

One could almost say that from time immemorial human beings have been making paint. Remnants of pigments and grinding tools have been discovered at some of the oldest known archaeological sites (Henshilwood et al. 2018) and in contexts indicating that various shades of ocher were used to adorn clothing and the human body itself. During this long tradition, paints were prepared from two main ingredients—a pigment and a binder—although sometimes a third ingredient, referred to as an extender, was included. The pigment was usually an inorganic mineral such as ocher, which was the source of various shades of yellow, red, and deep orange or brown. Calcium-rich clays produced white, and black pigment usually consisted of either charcoal or manganese. Limited analysis of the less frequently occurring green and blue pigments has identified their sources as the minerals celadonite and fuchsite. Green iron oxides and some plant-based dyes account for additional colors.

Mineralogically, ochers are a mixture of ferric oxide and other materials such as quartz and gypsum. Sourcing ochers is difficult, but because the associated additives vary among iron oxide sources, it is possible to identify individual ocher mines (Popelka-Filcoff 2006; Popelka-Filcoff et al. 2008). For example, the ocher at the La Prele Mammoth site was successfully sourced to the Sunrise ocher mine on the Hartville Uplift in eastern Wyoming (Zarzycka et al. 2019). Similarly, the ocher in rock paintings has been successfully sourced to various outcrops (Velliky and Reimer 2013).

Prehistoric artisans intentionally added binders or extending agents to ochers to prolong the attachment of their paints to stone surfaces and to reduce the required amount of pigment. This is another reason that the chemical composition of different paints is often unique, increasing the likelihood that different ocher sources can be traced and that different combinations of ingredients can help distinguish separate painting episodes at a site (Loendorf and Loendorf 2013).

Binders were almost always organic substances that evaporated as the paint dried, which makes them much more difficult to identify.

It is assumed that animal fat and bone grease, fish roe, eggs, and tree sap were among the binders included in prehistoric paints (Domingo and Chieli 2021). Some important experiments have revealed that the saponins in yucca-infused water may have been used to liquify pigments, making them easier to apply (Boyd and Dering 2013).[1]

Extenders, on the other hand, are thought to have consisted of crushed sand or neutral-colored clays that were added to augment the amount of pigment in a paint. Some studies suggest that crushed mica was added to make the paint shiny. There is evidence at one site in Montana that crushed bone was added to the paint (Loendorf and Scott-Cummings 2016).

Using pXRF

A pXRF instrument measures, in parts per million, the various constituents present in rock paintings. Sourcing red and yellow ochers and identifying individual batches of paint at pictograph sites are two applications of the technology. Another simpler but informative task is distinguishing between one set of black paintings at a site that have a charcoal pigment base and another set for which manganese was the source of the pigment (Castañeda et al. 2019). The results of pXRF analyses are frequently displayed in the form of graphs illustrating the mineral constituents of the paint sample, or spectra, in relation to one another.

One recent project used pXRF to identify and radiocarbon date a smoke-stained ceiling in a rockshelter and then compare the date with that of the sooty smoke adhering to the rockshelter's paintings (Rowe et al. 2021). In the following Step 8, "Establishing the Age of Rock Art," the use of pXRF instruments to assign relative ages to petroglyphs is discussed. Almost certainly this technology will be used in conjunction with other portable analytical methods for examining the composition of materials, such as Raman spectroscopy, for future rock art analysis.

Several companies make portable pXRF instruments, and although the Bruker Tracer analyzers are popular and reliable, they are expensive compared to other instruments that work just as well. Some analysts measure their target samples by handholding

1. See also https://shumla.org/experimental-archaeology-paint-making/.

FIGURE 7.1. Using a pXRF instrument on a tripod. The tripod makes it possible to set the instrument immediately adjacent to the painting but not touching it. It is also better for longer count times, when handholding the instrument can be tiresome. Photograph by Chris Loendorf.

their instruments, but if it is possible, a better result is produced by mounting the instrument on an adjustable tripod. This allows the nosepiece aperture to be placed immediately adjacent to the assayed rock surface and ensures stability during measurement. Even though the instruments weigh only 4 to 5 pounds, it is difficult to hold one in place for the required 100 to 150 seconds of count time, during which a person's arm may tire and allow the contact point to slip, producing inaccurate results. Count times vary, but, in general, the longer the count, the more accurate the result. Another advantage of using a tripod mount is that the instrument can be positioned immediately adjacent to the cliff surface and still not touch it. Site managers are vigilant when pXRF instruments are being used, but they are usually satisfied if they see the instrument can be positioned so the metal does not touch the painting.

X-rays penetrate the rock underlying the painting to a depth of up to approximately 4 millimeters, allowing control readings from the

FIGURE 7.2. Chris Loendorf using a handheld pXRF instrument while Bryan Medchill operates the computer. Sometimes it is not possible to set up a tripod, or even get one to a site, so pXRF instruments often need to be handheld. We place a pad, like the kind used for foot blisters, on the end of the instrument so the metal never touches the rock surface. Photograph by Lawrence Loendorf.

surrounding unpainted rock surface. When possible, a control data point near the pigment reading is collected for each sampled location within the painted areas. Often, however, time constraints make it necessary to limit the number of rock surface readings, and the subsequent analyses are based on grouped control readings.

It should be clear that pXRF data collection and analysis is not a simple point-and-shoot process. After collection, the data must be downloaded from the instrument to a laptop computer, which is usually straightforward but may become complicated. Once the data are successfully downloaded, it can be difficult to sort out the spectra and find meaningful results. Most rock art paintings in North America are red and made from ochers, so finding that there is a lot of iron in the sample does not help differentiate one red painting from another. The presence and identification of secondary minerals, perhaps due to impurities in the ocher or from an extender used in the paint, become important.

The focus of many rock art paint studies will be on unusual colors such as green, but the fact that the spectra include copper or chromium does not mean any mineral that was used to make the paint can be identified. In one study, SSR was able to suggest that the green was from fuchsite, or green mica, and then identify available sources of fuchsite in the vicinity of the paintings (Newman and Loendorf 2005:278). Identifying pigment mineral is not always easy though, and in many cases an analyst suggests only a possible source material.

Experiments with the use of combined pXRF and portable Raman spectroscopy have resulted in the identification of the ingredients in rock art paint. In a study at Hueco Tanks, Texas, that was mainly focused on learning the makeup of graffiti paint for subsequent removal by lasers, a few of the site's pictographs were included in the analysis (Lins et al. 2011). There are also ongoing experiments, discussed in Step 8, using pXRF instruments to establish relative ages for the rock varnish that accumulates on petroglyphs. Together, these efforts demonstrate that the potential for future use of pXRF technology in rock art research is excellent.

STEP 8

Establishing the Age of Rock Art

We have used the word "researchers" numerous times to refer to the people trying to learn about the nature and significance of the images that appear on rock surfaces. Archaeological research differs from structured learning in the other sciences, which require observing events occurring in the here and now—in a petri dish, in a kidney, in a nearby galaxy. The human beings that created rock art lived in the distant past, so what archaeologists observe are the results of past creative efforts. Making secure statements about a past that cannot be observed involves a process of reasoning called inference, embodied in an argument taking the form of "if this, then that."

Rock art researchers Christopher Chippindale and Paul Taçon were thinking about problems with dating rock art when they discussed the ideas expressed by Alison Wylie in her essay about archaeological reasoning (Taçon and Chippendale 1998; Wylie 1989). Wylie, a philosopher of science with a particular interest in archaeology, has observed that archaeological inference is often based upon chains of evidence built by adding one link to another ("if this, then that, and if that, then this and this"). The problem with this approach is that any chain is only as strong as its weakest link, and if one of the inferences in the chain is demonstrated to be false, then the argument so constructed falls apart. If, on the other hand, inferential arguments are constructed using several different types of evidence that together create an intellectual cable, and if the strands of evidence combine to form a strong cable, then it will not be broken when one thread is later discovered to be weak.

Numerical Estimates of Age

Because dating rock art is not a straightforward process, but instead can be difficult and complex, the researcher must use every piece of evidence, both numerical estimates as well as arguments of relatedness, referred to as relative estimates, to support a claim about the age of an image or panel. By doing so, the chance that the age is accurate is increased. Numerical estimates of age produce an estimated age in years, while relative estimates result from comparing properties of one or more figures to other similar figures of known age. Numerical estimates were once referred to as absolute dates, but archaeologists stopped using the term "absolute" because of an awareness of the presence of error factors in the dating process. As a result, calculations of the age of cultural remains are usually expressed as falling within a particular range, signifying that even though the estimate reflects a "no more than or less than" date, there is a high probability that it is correct. Tree-ring dating is one of the most accurate methods, but it has limited application in archaeological research and is essentially not useful for dating rock art.

Plasma Oxidation Dating

If a rock art site contains paintings, the figures may be suitable for radiocarbon dating using the plasma oxidation technique developed by Marvin Rowe and colleagues (Hyman and Rowe 1997a, 1997b; Rowe 2001; Russ et al. 1990). This process requires only a very small sample of pigment for analysis, and collection results in minimal damage to the rock art, especially when the sample is taken from an already damaged or incomplete image.

Using plasma oxidation dating, numerous Pecos River style paintings have been analyzed and dated by researchers at the Shumla Archaeological Research and Education Center, and the step-by-step process is described on the Center's website.[1] Briefly, a small sample of paint is heated with a low-temperature plasma to release the organic material in the binder that holds the paint together. This

1. https://shumla.org/shumla-chem-lab-part1/.

FIGURE 8.1. Marvin Rowe's apparatus for plasma oxidation dating. A sample being processed is visible in the vacuum tube. Photograph by Marvin Rowe.

material is siphoned off and submitted to an accelerator mass spectrometer (AMS) laboratory for radiocarbon dating. A sample of the background rock is also analyzed by the same procedure to be certain that it was not the source of the organic matter.

The process is not foolproof. The most common reason for failure is that the background rock contains too much organic matter, making it impossible to determine whether the organic content of a pictograph derived from the paint or the rock. Insufficient organic material in the sample is another reason that a sample cannot be dated. Nonetheless, using this method it is possible to successfully date rock art paint approximately 80 percent of the time. Direct dating of rock art pigments using the plasma oxidation method has successfully clarified and refined the dates of major rock art styles in Texas, New Mexico, Arizona, Montana, and Wyoming. The geology of a site appears to be a factor since the method appears to work better on limestone and rocks derived from volcanic activity than it does on sandstones.

Another strand in the cable of evidence used to date rock art comes from a method for obtaining the age of oxalates, which are naturally occurring compounds present in many types of plants, among them the metabolized fungi and lichens found on rock surfaces. Oxalates can be found over or under a rock painting and can be extracted and subjected to radiocarbon dating (Rowe and Steelman 2003; Steelman et al. 2021). The resulting numerical age can then be compared with the plasma oxidation date of the paint sample, adding considerable confidence to the date of the painting.

There are three low-energy plasma oxidation laboratories in North America: one directed by Marvin Rowe at the Office of Archaeological Studies in Santa Fe, New Mexico; one directed by Karen Steelman at the Shumla Center in Comstock, Texas; and the third directed by Ruth Ann Armitage at the Department of Chemistry at Eastern Michigan University in Ypsilanti. Samples are dated at a cost of approximately $1,000, although there are additional costs if a technician from one of the labs collects the sample(s) on-site.

Radiocarbon dating of the soot that often occurs on rockshelter ceilings is another technique for establishing the accuracy of a plasma oxidation date (Rowe et al. 2021). This method is limited to settings where pictographs or petroglyphs are themselves covered in soot, or where they were created on a soot-covered surface. Since it is easy to conclude that a rockshelter's walls are smoke-stained when actually the black stain is manganese, an initial step is to subject the residue to portable X-ray fluorescence (pXRF) analysis. Once it has been established that the residue is soot, a sample of the soot-covered rock is sent to a laboratory where the soot is removed in layers and radiocarbon dated. These dates are then correlated with the results of the plasma oxidation ages assigned to the rock art. Agreement between the dates produced by each process demonstrates the utility of building a reliable chain of evidence.

In instances in which a rock art figure or panel has been covered by mud from an adobe structure that had once adhered to a cliff wall, radiocarbon dating can provide another relative dating method by analyzing the fibers or binding material present in the mud. The adobe remnants usually cover the paintings, so their age is more recent than the artwork, but there are examples of images that were painted over the mud as well (Loendorf 2010).

Uranium-thorium (U-Th) dating, also called uranium-series dating, is a radiometric dating technique that measures the transformation over time of isotopes of uranium-234 to those of thorium-230 in a sample containing the chemical compound calcium carbonate ($CaCO_3$) and its crystalline variant, calcite. U-Th dating produces an analysis of the ratio of the two isotopes in the sample—less uranium and more thorium, for instance—from which an age in years can be estimated. U-Th dating has been applied mainly to travertine lakebed deposits, so its use for dating rock art paintings is new and experimental.

Under certain hydrologic conditions in the past, however, thin calcite layers have formed over rock art images, and U-Th dating has been used to establish the age of calcite deposits on cave paintings in Spain (Hoffmann et al. 2018) and Sulawesi, Indonesia (Brumm et al. 2021). A limitation of the technique is that a painting must lie under calcite or carbonate formations, and finding paintings that match this criterion is difficult. Researchers in North America have had more success in dating oxalates that over- or underlie rock paintings.

Radiocarbon dating of oxalates, soot, and fibers produces a numerical age in terms of "years ago," but the results are relative since the dated material is superimposed over or subimposed under the petroglyphs and pictographs. Nonetheless, in combination with other strands of evidence, they provide support for a reliable estimate of the age of the rock art.

Superimposition

The placement of one rock art image over another, or superimposition, can help to establish the age of the figures at a site in several ways. Most reliably, the placement of one recognizable motif over another identifiable motif can allow inferences about their ages. For example, if images of a horse or a gun are superimposed over the figure of a quadruped that is itself superimposed over a bow and arrow, it is reasonable to infer that the image of the quadruped is younger than the bow and arrow but older than the horse or gun. In some parts of North America, the time frame for the creation of these images could be relatively short. Unfortunately, such neat superimpositions are not common and require rock art researchers to be creative.

FIGURE 8.2. Rahman Abdullayev using a digital microscope to study the superimposition of paint layers at a site near Las Cruces, New Mexico. Photograph by Lawrence Loendorf.

One approach is to examine the composition, application technique, and color of the paint used in pictographs. It is often possible to determine if paint was applied with a finger, a brush, or a lump of dry pigment, and once these different techniques have been identified, the type of paint applied can be determined (Greer 1995; Greer and Greer 2021). For example, the superimposition of red-painted images that have been brushed over a black figure that was created using a dry charcoal lump results from two application techniques that can be sorted out. Using pXRF analysis to identify the composition of different batches of paint can supplement the evidence from the superimposition of the images on the rock surface and support judgments about the sequence and temporal placement of the images.

Determining which paint is superimposed over another is not always straightforward, especially when the underlying color is dense and solid, and the overlying color is lighter and not highly pigmented. White paint sometimes does not adhere well to underlying black pigments, and sometimes the darker black color is visible through

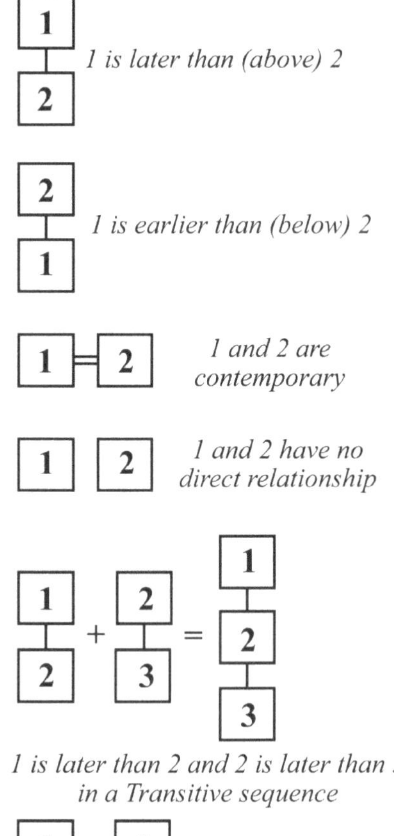

FIGURE 8.3. Rules for making a Harris diagram to study superimposition at a site. Adapted from Loubser 1997.

the overlying white color. Digital microscopes connected to a laptop computer or smartphone can help determine which color is on top of another. Usually, if the paint is magnified, specks of an overlying color can become visible on an underlying one.

The images produced by microscopes are also helpful in studying instances of superimposition of petroglyphs. Determining the order of superimposition of pecked petroglyphs is best accomplished by analyzing the development of rock varnish, which is usually greater on the underlying figure. The superimposition of incised petroglyphs associated with pecked ones can be easier to sort out if the incising is deep, whereas shallow marks or scratches can be hard to evaluate.

Archaeologists use Harris diagrams "to graphically represent complex three-dimensional superpositioning, or stratification, between paintings on a two-dimensional surface" (Loubser 1997:3). Descriptions of how to construct Harris diagrams are available online.[2] Essentially, they are based on the principle that a unit closer to the surface, and referred to as Unit 1, is more recent than a unit occurring deeper (Unit 2). Therefore, if Unit 3 is deeper than Unit 2, it is also older than Unit 1. If at some locations at a site, Unit 1 is found to be older than Unit 2, then the units are said to be contemporary because the stratigraphic relationship between two points at a larger site can change, as the diagrams are designed to display. Loubser (1997) makes clear that the study of superimposition can only be done in the field, where it is possible to examine the rock images physically. Originally developed for analyzing and depicting the complex stratigraphy at historic sites, Harris diagrams were initially applied to a rock art site in Australia (Chippindale and Taçon 1993). Subsequently described by Loubser (1997), Harris diagrams are now a regular part of research at rock art sites featuring superimposed images.

Relative Dating of Petroglyphs Using Associated Well-dated Deposits

Artifacts of a known age and excavated deposits that have been radiocarbon dated and occur adjacent to a panel of figures can help to establish the age of nearby rock art. Although the images have not been directly dated, the additional archaeological materials are evidence that at least one person was present at the site contemporaneously with the creation of the rock art. The reverse is also true. Some rock art styles are so well known that they have been used as indicators of the location of archaeological deposits. Early investigators in the American Southwest searched for panels of Basketmaker rock art when they wanted to find and excavate Basketmaker sites.

2. See, for example, https://en.wikipedia.org/wiki/Harris_matrix.

Analysis of the changes in the topography of a landscape can sometimes provide chronological evidence of the time frame during which a rock art site was created. When a panel of images occurs several meters above the base of a canyon wall that was cut by the river flowing below it, it may be possible to determine the age of the soil surface that originally allowed access to the panel surface if the development of the river's geological terraces has been studied. This approach was used at a site on the Powder River in Wyoming, where thermoluminescence dating and radiocarbon dates for a local river terrace were used together to successfully determine the level where individuals in the past would have created the panel of rock paintings (Castañeda et al. 2021:13).

A more common setting is one where rock art images are fully or partially buried by soil deposits. Rock art panels that are oriented toward the sky on a flat bedrock surface are often covered with soil and remain undiscovered because investigators are inspecting cliff walls instead of ground-level surfaces. A good example of buried petroglyphs occurred at a site on Glorieta Mesa near Santa Fe, New Mexico (Abel 1993; Loendorf 2008). The recording crew used whisk brooms to clean the rock art panels, discovering in the process that many of the petroglyphs were buried under sandy soil that was between 25 and 30 centimeters deep. They were assisted by John C. Phillips, a Forest Service soil specialist, who was able to determine that the overlying soils were well developed. There were significant clay and calcium carbonate accumulations at the bottom of the soil profiles, which meant that the soils were old and had not just washed in during a flood event.

The ages of the petroglyphs at the Glorieta Mesa site were established by a series of radiocarbon dates on the soil samples overlying the panels. A sample from 15 centimeters above the petroglyph panel was dated to 2570 ± 70 BC, while another sample from 4 centimeters above the panel had a date of 4480 ± 70 BC. Since the samples were taken from a well-developed soil profile, the dates indicate that the petroglyphs are more than 5,000 years old.

Another excellent example of dating petroglyphs by learning the age of associated soils comes from the Long Lake site in Oregon, where a panel of abstract petroglyphs was covered by a layer of Mazama ash (Ricks 1995). The ash, or tephra, was ejected from Mount

Mazama in southern Oregon approximately 7,600 years ago, which means that the underlying petroglyphs are at least 7,600 years old. The resulting collapsed caldera is the site of today's Crater Lake. The petroglyphs from Long Lake are now referred to as examples of the Great Basin Abstract/Carved style and are acknowledged to be among the oldest dated petroglyphs in North America (Middleton et al. 2014).

Researchers working on another important dating project at Winnemucca Lake, Nevada, were able to date a layer of carbonates that had developed over Great Basin Abstract/Carved style petroglyphs to an age of more than 10,500 years (Benson et al. 2013).

Another strand of relevant dating information resulted from the coring of the ancient lakebed, enabling the researchers to establish that the old lake had filled and drained at different times in the past. Using these data, it was possible to determine when the petroglyph boulders would have been either underwater or exposed and accessible for carving—in this instance, between 13,000 and 14,000 years ago. These results provide an instructive example of the utility of using more than one method to establish the age of a rock art site.

Problems with Numerical Dating of Petroglyphs

Dating petroglyphs using relative techniques such as superimposition and soil analysis has been productive, but there is not yet a reliable method for determining the numerical ages of petroglyphs. Unfortunately, two once-promising techniques, weathering rind organics (WRO) and cation-ratio (CR) dating, have been abandoned because of their potential to produce incorrect ages (Dorn 1997; Welsh and Dorn 1997). In some instances, however, CR dates can be used as relative ages, so it can be worth the effort invested in obtaining them (Loendorf 2018).

Varnish microlamination (VML) is another method that has been used successfully to date petroglyphs. Microlaminations occur in the coating, commonly referred to as rock varnish, that usually develops in layers on exposed rock surfaces in arid environments. The composition varies in response to environmental changes, so in arid periods, a varnish layer will contain more iron, while in wetter conditions, the varnish contains more manganese. The thin layers can be correlated with local climatic events, making it possible for an investigator to determine if the varnish on a petroglyph preceded a wet pluvial period or an extended hot, dry interval.

Some of the drawbacks of using the VML method to date petroglyphs include, first, the fact that the resultant date is only a minimum age and is often not very precise. Researchers are aware that there have been long periods of drought in prehistory, but the exact dates of a relevant dry period are often a work in progress. Second, VML dating requires an experienced specialist, with skills that are not widely available, to remove and analyze the sample. The third problem is that rock varnish does not always contain laminations, which, if none are found, can result in a fruitless and expensive trip to the field by a specialist. Nonetheless, if a specialist is available and a program for dating rock art in a region is underway, it is worthwhile to invest in obtaining VNL dates.

Rock Varnish Estimates

Even though using rock varnish to estimate the age of petroglyph figures can be problematic, researchers have learned to maximize the information available in less than perfect circumstances. A basic rule of thumb is that petroglyphs on which the varnish has accumulated to the density and darkness of the surrounding rock wall are obviously older than those that are lightly varnished. One exception to this generalization is the fact that varnish does not accumulate at the same rate, so one section of a panel can be more heavily varnished than another. Additionally, varnish that was once thick can erode from the petroglyph surface, making it appear younger than its actual age. Fortunately, an experienced researcher can usually detect these inconsistencies and find places on the petroglyph that are unaffected by diminished varnish development.

When working on large recording projects, SSR recorders assign a number from 1 to 10 that corresponds to the amount of varnish observed. A totally unvarnished figure receives a 1, while a figure completely darkened with varnish is designated a 10. The same person is responsible for evaluating the varnish level at the entire site to ensure that the estimates are based on the same criteria. Consistent determinations are especially important in the midrange estimates of between 4 and 7. The data summarizing the degree of varnish cover become part of the site record and are used in additional analyses.

Ongoing experimental research is focused on the use of pXRF instruments to measure the amounts of manganese and iron, which are the main constituents of rock varnish. Meinrat Andreae and colleagues (2020) undertook the initial research in Saudi Arabia, where they were analyzing the composition of historic inscriptions of known age. Inscriptions in an ancient Thamudic script on rock outcrops have been dated to 1200 BC, and there are many others on outcrops from more recent times. Using pXRF instruments, researchers were able to measure the amount of manganese and iron in the varnish covering the inscriptions, thereby establishing the rate of accumulation of these minerals in the varnish covering nearby petroglyphs.

The studies in Saudi Arabia are significant, but the technique is not applicable to inscriptions in the Americas, which are seldom older than a few hundred years, an insufficient amount of time for varnish to develop, and for researchers to establish an accumulation rate. Nonetheless, Andreae and colleagues (Andreae and Andreae 2022) have established a relatively uniform rate for the growth of manganese on rock surfaces in California, Nevada, Utah, Wyoming, and Montana. This research will require considerably more testing, but if there is a linear rate of manganese deposition on petroglyphs that can be measured and compared to the amount of manganese in the background rock varnish, this technique will be extremely useful for the relative dating of petroglyphs.

Clearly, VML dating and the use of pXRF to determine the amount of manganese in rock varnish are experimental techniques, but the results they are producing are encouraging and should motivate researchers to continue to study methods for dating petroglyphs.

For readers who want to learn more about rock art dating, Marymore and Rowe (2021) provide a list of relevant articles discussing dating studies.

STEP 9

Laboratory Work and Research

Rock art researchers have estimated that every hour they spend doing fieldwork necessitates four to five hours of laboratory work and site write-up. During this step, all the collected data included in survey forms, photographs, illustrations, and maps, as well as any specialized analysis, are processed in off-site laboratory settings.

Refining and Photographing the Field Drawings

A significant effort is invested in finalizing and inking the field drawings and tracings of the rock art panels, after which they are photographed to produce a digital image. As described previously in "Step 4: Panel Forms, Measured Drawings, and Tracings," the panel tracings are recorded on acetate film, so photography can proceed in several ways. After a scale is placed on the films, they can be hung in a photographic studio against a white backdrop in front of a strobe light. This setup provides the same kind of illumination as placing the film on a light box. Alternately, the film can simply be hung in good light and photographed. If there are several small film tracings from the same panel, they can be photocopied and then fitted together to make a final drawing that can then be photographed with a digital camera. Producing an accurate final digital copy requires that the scale at which the traced figures were recorded is identical.

The digital photos are then assembled and digitally rectified in Photoshop using registration marks on the film to align and correct

FIGURE 9.1. Laurie White using a tablet connected to a computer to complete a panel drawing. Photograph by Laurie White.

overlapping pieces. Field photographs are often used as references to ensure correct alignment, after which Photoshop tools for lens distortion correction are applied. A sequence of separate layers is created for natural features, the paintings, surface abrasion, scale, and plumb line, which allows a recording artist to create and manipulate variations of an image. For instance, graffiti on a panel can be included in one version but removed from another. Field photographs are placed on the transparent background for reference and checking throughout the process.

After the layers are created, a Wacom digital drawing tablet or similar device is used to retrace and refine the original traced images or field drawings, after which they are saved as high-resolution, layered TIFF files and as one-layer JPEG files. Hard copies of the illustrations will be printed on 8½ × 11-inch paper and inserted in the final report along with the survey forms.

Design Element Inventory

Geometric

Dots

2a	Single or forked line	2c	Clustered dots	2e	Life form
2b	Grouped or parallel lines	2d	Geometric form	2z	See PDS

Lines, Open

1a	Single straight line	1x	T-shape	1v	Incurved X
1b	Parallel straight lines	1k	Single zigzag	1dd	Lines from point
1d	One-pole ladder	1l	Parallel zigzag group	1bb	Asterisk
1e	Rake	9d	Lightning	1g	Forked line
1u	Rake with wavy line	1m	Rectilinear meander	1h	Branched line
1i	Angled line / chevron	1n	Rectilinear scroll	1cc	Trident
1j	Parallel angled lines	1c	Cross or X	1w	See PDS

Lines, Closed

3r	Simple triangle	3o	Grouped / joined rectangles	9a	Star
3s	Hourglass	1f	Two-pole ladder	3aa	Outlined cross
3t	Joined triangles / sawtooth	3n	Gridded rectangle	3u	Stepped triangle
3w	Elaborated triangle	3ee	Open grid	3v	Terraced pyramid
3cc	Vulva form	3y	Elaborated rectangle	9f	Cloud terrace
3l	Rectangle / square	3p	Diamond		
3m	Concentric rectangles	3q	Grouped / joined diamonds	1za	See PDS

Lines Curved, Open

1o	Curved line / arc	1y	U-shape	1s	Curvilinear meander
1p	Parallel curved lines / arc /rainbow	1q	Wavy line	1t	Spiral or scroll
1aa	Hooked line	1r	Grouped wavy line	1zb	See PDS

FIGURE 9.2. The initial page of the design element types used by the Archaeological Society of New Mexico Rock Art Council. When selecting a category code from this chart, it is important to match the text description to the element being recorded. The drawings are just possible examples, not an exhaustive list, and they may not correspond to the element being recorded even though the text description is accurate.

Future developments in computer hardware and software technology will undoubtedly introduce more efficient, less time-consuming techniques for working with field tracings and drawings.

Typology

Tabulating the kinds and numbers of elements found at a site is another step done in the laboratory. In Step 4, we noted that some state agencies require the use of standardized element identification sheets that are completed in the field. If this requirement applies, then these sheets should be used to classify the individual rock art motifs. In locations lacking a prescribed typology, the researcher must create an original classification.

Developing a typology for rock art is similar to developing a structured order of other archaeological entities. Categories are specified based on the attributes that the researcher has determined are essential to defining the types of figures present at the site. These attributes can vary, but the shape or form of each petroglyph element is always included. Representational elements are usually described separately from abstract forms.

For example, the criteria for defining abstract forms could include the following descriptions:

> A *circle* is a circular or ovoid form that encloses unfilled space. The circle does not have to close, but it should be at least 95 percent complete. Erosion can cause some portion of a circle to be missing, although some circles are intentionally left unfinished.
>
> A *bisected rectangle* is an unfilled square or rectangular form divided by an interior line that may extend beyond the perimeter of the figure.

There are dozens of other abstract forms that require similar definitions, but often it is possible to rely on an existing typology developed during prior research.

As also noted in Step 4, the use of element categories is not encouraged during field recording because doing so can exclude a possibly more accurate later identification of the figure. Once laboratory work begins, however, categories can be useful, especially if additional criteria are developed to clarify inconsistencies. At this stage, classification should be the work of only one person to ensure consistency in the criteria used to assign elements to groups of types.

In addition to form and shape, other attributes that might contribute to a classification system include an image's size, the size of the panel in which the figures occur, the percentage of the panel surface covered by rock art, the depth of the petroglyphs, the color of the paint, and relative estimates of the degree of varnish cover. Written criteria developed for descriptive categories such as circles and curvilinear meanders are strictly applied, and once the system accounts for all known variability, a series of figure types is established.

Workable typologies are used for a variety of tasks, foremost among them the comparison of petroglyph and pictograph types at different sites as the first step in identifying regional petroglyph and pictograph styles. In many places, previous research has already established a region's rock art styles, so the task in the laboratory is to determine which previously defined styles are represented in the panels of the recently recorded site.

Seriation

Seriation has been used to establish regional rock art chronologies in several parts of North America, and it is another useful procedure to apply after rigorous types have been developed. A basic assumption of frequency seriation is that artifact types—in this case, categories of rock art figures—have the equivalent of a life cycle. The frequencies of a type, such as circular forms, will be low at Point A in time, then gradually increase to maximum popularity at Point B, and begin to decrease as another type, introduced at Point C, begins its own ascending trajectory.

Inconsistency is the biggest problem affecting the development of rock art seriation. If more than one researcher is responsible for classifying petroglyph figures, one person might identify a figure as "interconnected lines," whereas someone else might classify the same figure as a "stick anthropomorph." Even if the criteria for each element in a typology are unambiguous, individual bias can still influence the classification and seriation process.

Seriation is useful as a relative dating method when it is combined with other chronological methods. Correlating each of the dating methods used at the site is a significant part of the laboratory research and, combined with a discussion about the distribution of the rock art, is presented in a section on the site's age in the final report.

Distribution

Although there are a number of ways to study the distribution of rock art, four main approaches predominate, differing primarily in the scale of analytical focus (Whitley and Loendorf 2005). The first level of analysis examines the relationship between two or more figures in a panel to identify patterns creating an intentional composition or scene, or a more general symbolic association. For example, a scene may consist of a horse and a human figure made by the same technique. In such a case, it is possible to establish a contemporaneous relationship between the horse and the human, suggesting that the maker intended for them to be juxtaposed. In other instances, however, the association is not obvious and can only be identified through a method that reveals a pattern or reoccurrence. Alternatively, some associations between motifs may be intentional but non-compositional. These require multiple examples, from more sites, to sort out what they might mean, in the sense that the creation of visually coherent scenes was not intended.

A second level of analysis examines the relationship between rock art and other archaeological features or components of a site. These may include additional rock art panels, but in many cases rock art figures are situated in relation to architecture or other archaeological features. This intrasite level of analysis can be useful in identifying activity or specialized task areas within a site.

The third important scale of analysis is the examination of rock art sites in relation to one another. At this intersite level, it may be possible to identify the distribution of images that are common across a region and to establish types or styles of rock art and the geographic boundaries that separate them. The results of this research may be able to support inferences about former social or political units.

Pictograph and petroglyph sites are also studied in relation to the landscapes in which they occur. This fourth scale can vary from the level of the panel, where relationships between motifs and natural rock features are investigated; to the site level, where the area within the viewshed of a rock art site is examined; and to the regional level, where the locations of sites are examined within their geographical context.

As with many heuristic systems, these approaches are not always mutually exclusive. For instance, images are frequently connected by lines, or simply by a shared attribute, to cracks or holes in the rock surface. As such, they are related to the environment or the substrate and might logically be included in a landscape approach to studying rock images, or in a study at the intraregional scale as well.

Ethnography

The involvement of Native consultants has increasingly become a significant part of rock art research. In Robert Layton's (2001:316) excellent summary of the principles of ethnographic practice at rock art sites, he identifies several levels of research. The most immediate contribution comes from local groups or tribes who consult at the site and share their insights. Experience has shown that even if contemporary tribal people do not have specific information about the rock art images, they retain traditional knowledge about properties of the site's setting or surroundings, such as the presence of medicinal plants.

The effect of the American Indian Religious Freedom Act of 1978, a United States federal law, and other laws focused on historic preservation has been to reverse prohibitions against the presence of Native Americans at sacred sites containing rock art, and to encourage their participation in on-site research. In many instances, governmental land-managing agencies have interviewed Native consultants standing before panels containing petroglyphs and paintings, and if the information provided is not considered proprietary, it may be available when recording the site.

If direct input from Native consultants is not available, researchers need to rely on the existing ethnographic record, which is seldom a straightforward process. Commenting on the lack of ethnographic descriptions of rock art sites, South African archaeologist David Lewis-Williams has emphasized that when approaching the ethnographic literature, "you need to read it, reread it, and read it again" (personal communication between Lewis-Williams and Loendorf, May 3, 1987). Lewis-Williams means that the production of rock art is invariably related to other aspects of a group's lifeways, and that from a study of their subsistence and related practices, an understanding of their rock art may emerge. For example, if a group enhances their success in hunting by extensive use of sympathetic or imitative magic, it is probable that their rock art would include pictures of animals pierced by arrows.

The ledger drawings and other illustrations made by Plains individuals, primarily on paper, have been sources of relevant information about biographic and/or narrative rock art panels at Plains and Great Basin archaeological sites where representational and abstract images occur on several different kinds of surfaces. Similarly, the numerous and varied designs painted on Mimbres ceramics are examples of how imagery can be helpful in interpreting rock art from the Mogollon region of the American Southwest. Kiva wall paintings and drawings on house walls are also important sources of relevant imagery.

A number of ceremonial figures that have been depicted in ceramic form and in a variety of materials—for example, the long-nosed deity masks made of bone, copper, and whelk shell associated with the Mississippian culture in the American Midwest—are also recognizable in rock art. These and other examples illustrate that the ethnographic and archaeological records often contain similar or identical images, and that a careful study of the former can reliably inform the interpretation of the latter.

In settings for which there is no available ethnographic record to consult, it is sometimes possible to extrapolate from the ethnography of neighboring groups, particularly if they belong to the same language family. But even when adjacent tribes speak different languages, they may have adapted to their environment in similar ways. Of course, the ethnography of hunters and gatherers will be more applicable to another group with similar lifeways than it would be for agriculturally based peoples.

Neuropsychological Models

In their landmark article introducing the neuropsychological (N-P) model, Lewis-Williams, Dowson and colleagues (1988) precede their interpretation of certain kinds of rock art with the observation that the human brain generates a range of luminous perceptions that are independent of light from an external source (see Whitley and

Loendorf 2005 for an expanded discussion). These visual phenomena generally take geometric forms such as grids, zigzags, dots, and spirals, and are experienced as shimmering, moving, rotating, and sometimes enlarging patterns that grade into one another and combine in bewildering arrays. This imagery is induced by many means, including sensory deprivation, intense concentration, intense auditory stimuli, and rhythmic movement (Horowitz 1964; Klüver 1942; Siegel and Jarvik 1975), all of which can create altered states of consciousness (ASCs).

Other researchers (e.g., Hedges 1982) had previously linked these visual images to petroglyphs and pictographs, but Lewis-Williams, Dowson, and colleagues (1988:203–204) expanded the model to include three basic stages that appear in the progression of mental imagery during trance states. Beginning with the perception of simple geometric shapes, which they termed "entoptics," subjects then try to make sense of the images by interpreting them as recognizable forms. In other words, the brain attempts to construe the perceived images as culturally meaningful. The final stage marks the transition to full hallucinations in which the images are often associated with culturally influenced items, memories, or powerful emotional experiences. These visions are often projected onto a background of the entoptics, and the imagery increases in vividness.

This research is particularly important because it is based on an argument of universality: All humans share the same neuropsychological systems, and, for this reason, all react to ASCs in similar ways; humans are all similarly hardwired and share a definable range of mental, visual, and physical reactions to trance, regardless of how the trance is induced. This would mean that the neuropsychological principles or regularities underlying trance states apply to people in all cultures, even though different cultures place different values or meanings on visionary experiences.

Critics of the N-P model claim that it is too monolithic to serve as an explanation for a large category of rock art images (e.g., Bahn 1988). Some argue that it can only reasonably be applied to the rock art of shamanistic societies (although it has been mistakenly applied to gardening groups that do not practice shamanism). In addition, the N-P model cannot properly be based on a single or small number of motifs, or on an examination of only a handful of characteristics.

The strongest inferences are based on a close fit between the model and images produced during the construal stage, when the entoptics, or abstract forms, are transposed into representational forms, indicating the trance state of rock art production.

The N-P model is not needed at rock art sites where imagery reflecting known shamanistic ideology—such as transformational human figures attached to duck heads, or figures that are half-human and half-bison—is recognizable (Halifax 1982; Loendorf and White 2021; Schaafsma 1994). Figures in transformational flight are also strong indicators of shamanism (Turpin 1994).

Collection of Prior Records and Photographs

The laboratory effort involving the collection of earlier site records and photographs for comparative purposes actually begins at the start of a project. The ongoing search continues for documents that are often found in the archives of libraries and historical societies, in computer searches, in collections of avocational photographs, and in museums and curation facilities. Many rock art sites were the subjects of earlier professional and avocational research, and these investigations can supply critical information, particularly about sites or panels within sites that have been vandalized, eroded, or otherwise destroyed. In many instances, earlier investigators collected artifacts from rockshelters containing rock art. These artifacts, often curated at museums or state and military curation facilities, may provide information about the age of the rock art.

STEP 10

Preparing the Site Report

The last step in recording a rock art site is the preparation of a comprehensive final report that includes the research findings and presents ideas about the affiliation of the rock art. The sometimes-varying views and interpretations of the rock art by Native American consultants are also incorporated as succinctly and accurately as possible. It is customary for Sacred Sites Research (SSR) archaeologists to prepare two reports: the primary one for the project sponsors and a second, shorter version for the public that includes the primary features of the site and many illustrations.

The report describes the work done at the site and usually includes the recording methods, a site map of the locations of all panels, plan-view maps showing the relationship of panels to one another, illustrations of each panel showing the individual elements, and photographs of the panels and elements with links to the panel drawings. If the project included a research design, it should appear in the final report.

Step 6: Site Mapping presents the procedure that SSR archaeologists follow to complete a spatial distribution analysis of the site, and the results of this work are an important part of the final report. The ages of individual figures, as well as the methods used to establish them, should be presented along with the implications these ages have for the site and other sites in the region.

Unless the site is already well known to the public, its precise location is usually omitted from reports having a wide distribution.

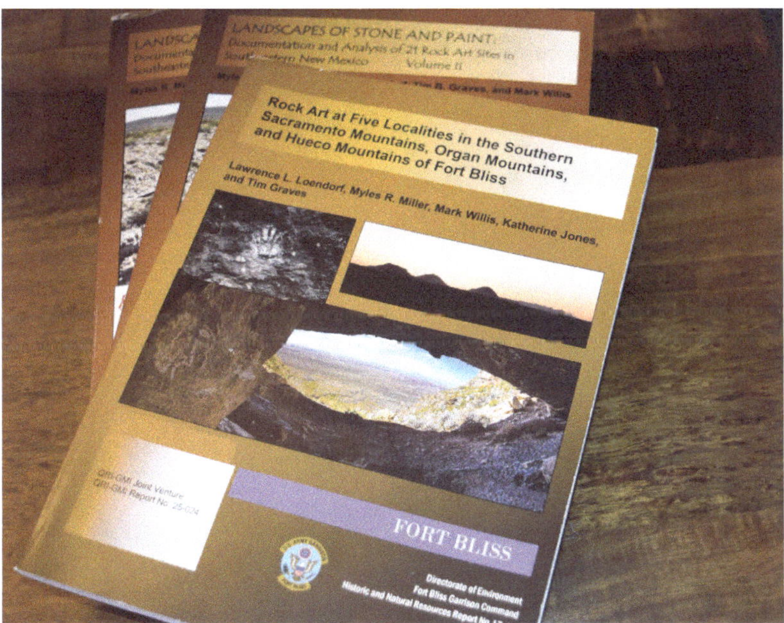

FIGURE 10.1. Final reports for rock art recording projects at sites in the Jornada Mogollon region of New Mexico and Texas. Photograph by Lawrence Loendorf.

Federal and state land-managing agencies, as well as private owners, may have specific rules about the release of site location data that must be observed in the final report. Even disclosing the site name can be problematic if it includes geographical features that can be easily identified. For example, instead of referring to the Turtle Butte site, the report should use a geographically nonspecific name such as the Cactus Patch site. Similarly, a better name for the Campbell Family Farm site would be the Painted Deer site.

The so-called archaeological gray literature—privately circulated reports such as summaries of fieldwork conducted by contract archaeologists—is extensive but often inaccessible, so publishing the results of rock art recording projects in journals, monographs, and books contributes valuable information to other researchers. Major archaeological journals such as *Kiva* and *Plains Anthropologist* regularly publish articles about rock art, although they usually focus on the age or distribution of a type or style. Site reports are more often published in the journals of local and state archaeological societies,

FIGURE 10.2. A popular report prepared for the landowners of a large site near Manila, Utah. Tour groups sometimes visit the site, so the goal of the report was to give visitors an opportunity to learn about rock art and the site. Photograph by Lawrence Loendorf.

and in the publications of the American Rock Art Research Association (ARARA). Articles submitted to *American Indian Rock Art* (*AIRA*), also published by ARARA, are reviewed by referees who are often willing to help new writers publish their work. Presenting the results of research at an ARARA national meeting can often be a prelude to its being published in *La Pintura*. Another venue for sharing information is the annual meeting of the Society for American Archaeology (SAA), which has a rock art interest group that sponsors symposia to which papers can be submitted. The SAA also provides the opportunity to display rock art images and an abstract of the accompanying site report in an area reserved for poster sessions.

Conclusions

Step-by-Step

We wrote this book to introduce our 10-step process of recording rock art. Our fieldwork was enlightened by the experience of researchers who preceded us, as well as by our own procedures when given the opportunity to record the images from the past that remain on rocks. We have many colleagues who pursue the same goals, and from our combined efforts many effective tools are continually being developed and used successfully.

We are not the first to discuss new rock art recording methods. "Recording Rock Art: Strategies, Challenges, and Embracing the Digital Revolution" is the title of a chapter by Liam Michael Brady, Jamie Hampson, and Inés Domingo Sanz (2017) in *The Oxford Handbook of the Archaeology and Anthropology of Rock Art*, edited by Bruno David and Ian J. McNiven. It does present up-to-date techniques for recording rock art, but the discussion is limited. A concise introduction to rock art recording is found in *Rock Art Recording Methods from Traditional to Digital*, by Inés Domingo Sanz (2020).

In 2018, Creighton Gerber completed a master's thesis at Northern Arizona University titled "Digital Recording and Interpretation of Rock Art at Walnut Canyon National Monument." Anyone interested in using multiple photographic techniques to study rock art sites would benefit from reviewing this thesis.[1]

1. Digital recording and interpretation of rock art at Walnut Canyon National Monument - OpenKnowledge@NAU.

Heather Morrison, also a Northern Arizona University student, completed a thesis titled "Portable X-ray Fluorescence Compositional Analysis and Recording Techniques of Pictographs at Canyon de Chelly National Monument." Morrison used a grid sampling strategy for collecting pXRF points, which makes her thesis, completed in 2020, an important addition to the literature on rock art recording.

Also in 2020, Belinda C. Mollard completed a dissertation at the University of Leicester titled "Understanding a Ritual Landscape: An Investigation Into the Rock Art of the Jornada Mogollon Region of the America Southwest." Mollard uses a "looking out" approach to the viewshed of rock art sites and possibly associated natural and cultural features and artifacts.

There is also information about rock art recording on the American Rock Art Research Association (ARARA) website. The discussion includes different examples of site data and panel recording forms. ARARA also offers scholarships to students interested in rock art studies, and many of the supported projects are related to innovative recording techniques.[2]

The Utah Rock Art Research Association (URARA) has many rock art recording projects and also has a grant program to support the recording of sites within the state.

The Shumla Archaeological and Education Center website has information about its scholar's program, which offers internships for students who want to learn in-field rock art recording methods, as well as laboratory internships for students working with dating methods.[3]

The Mesa Prieta Petroglyph Project focuses on the documentation and protection of the rock art of the northern Rio Grande Valley. Volunteers are encouraged to help with recording, and youth intern programs are offered.[4] The Archaeological Society of New Mexico Rock Art Council is an active group of rock art recorders with a long history of successfully working at sites across the state and is one of the better places to learn about rock art recording. The Council's website has information about how to learn to record rock art.[5]

2. www.arara.org.

3. www.shumla.org.

4. www.mesaprietapetroglyphs.org.

5. https://archaeologicalsocietynm.org/rock-art-council.

Every few years the Texas Archaeological Society offers academies on various archaeological topics. Individuals can sign up for a weekend of training in recording and research. The 10-step approach presented in this book was first introduced at a 2019 Texas Archaeological Society rock art academy in El Paso. Training sessions and field schools for recording rock art are also offered in other western, and some eastern, states.

Our most important conclusion is that interested individuals can find programs that teach rock art recording techniques, and we hope the steps discussed in this book will help in that discovery. The cultural resources that we have focused on, the pictographs and petroglyphs, need to be documented carefully and extensively if they are to survive and inspire future generations.

Appendix A:
SSR Rock Art Panel Form

SSR Rock Art Panel and Condition Assessment Form (New Mexico)

<table>
<tr><td colspan="3">ARMS Site #:
NMCRIS #</td><td colspan="3">Site name:</td></tr>
<tr><td colspan="2">Panel # of total panels</td><td colspan="2">Date:

Time:</td><td colspan="2">Weather:

Temp. & Relative Humidity:</td></tr>
<tr><td colspan="6">Panel location</td></tr>
<tr><td>Rockshelter:</td><td>Cliff face:</td><td colspan="2">Boulder:</td><td colspan="2">Other (explain below):</td></tr>
<tr><td colspan="6">Location description (provenience/position within the site and distance from nearest associated panel(s)):</td></tr>
<tr><td>GPS Data/UTMs:

Zone: Easting:</td><td colspan="2">NAD:

Northing:</td><td colspan="3">Aspect/Facing:

Angle:</td></tr>
<tr><td colspan="3">Panel Information</td><td colspan="3">Rock Type:</td></tr>
<tr><td colspan="6">Dimensions: Height: Width:

Height of lowest rock art element(s) above ground level:

Or, give the measurement of the soil deposits covering the lowest elements:

Height of highest rock art element(s) above ground level:

Other:</td></tr>
<tr><td colspan="6">Varnish Cover (mark with an "x" all that apply):</td></tr>
<tr><td>Low:</td><td colspan="2">Medium:</td><td colspan="2">Heavy:</td><td>Total:</td></tr>
<tr><td colspan="6"></td></tr>
<tr><td colspan="6">Motif Type and Method (mark with an "X" for all that apply)</td></tr>
<tr><td>Petroglyph
Stipple Pecked:
Solid Pecked:
Abraded:
Incised/Carved:
Scratched:
Drilled:</td><td colspan="2">Pictograph
Monochromatic:
Polychromatic:
Brush:
Stick/Pencil:
Charcoal:
Crayon:
Unknown:</td><td colspan="3">Parent Rock (Munsell):

Design color(s):

Design color(s):

Design color(s):</td></tr>
<tr><td colspan="6">Natural Rock Incorporation (explain):</td></tr>
<tr><td colspan="6">Superimposition (explain):</td></tr>
<tr><td colspan="6">Associated Natural/Cultural Features and Samples Collected (Describe)</td></tr>
<tr><td colspan="6">Features:

Bedrock mortars, metates, cupules:

Medicinal plants:

Samples:</td></tr>
</table>

Short Description of Panel and Element(s) (reference element categories; label a, b, c, etc., include size)

Age Estimation (*mark with an "X" all that apply*):					
Paleo-Indian:	Archaic:	Formative:	Proto-historic:	Historic:	Unknown:
Cultural Affiliation if Known (*explain*):					

Panel Condition					
Natural Deterioration and Threats (*mark with an "X" all that apply, and explain below*)					
Wash zones: Seeps: Damp areas:	Water related conditions: Soluble salts: Insoluble salts: Other (*explain below*):	Abrasion: Cleaving: Dust: Exfoliation: Granulation: Wind erosion:	Vegetation: Lichen: Partial: Overall:	Fungi: Mould: Algae:	Animals: Birds: Bats: Insects:
Description of Natural Deterioration:					

Intentional Forms of Cultural Deterioration					
Graffiti: (*mark with an "X" the type and form present, and describe below*)					
Initials: Inscription:	Symbols: Chalk:	Charcoal: Pencil:	Pen: M arker:	Paint: Spray:	Other (*explain*):
Description of Graffiti:					

Other Forms of Destruction Observed (*mark all that apply with an "X", and explain below*)	
Vandalism:	Site Visitation/Recreation Activities:
Gun shot:	Evidence of Rock Climbing:
Evidence of Pot Hunters:	Litter:
Livestock damage:	Camp fires:
Other artificial/cultural deterioration observed (*explain*):	
Description of Cultural Deterioration:	

Panel Integrity and Significance
Description of Panel Integrity (*as relates to design and workmanship*)**:**
Panel contributes to significance of the site (*explain*):
Natural/Cultural Concerns That May Continue to Threaten the Condition and Integrity of the Panel:
Management Recommendations:
Previous Investigations/Documentation:

Photograph Documentation (*insert details for all that apply, see Photo Log for additional information*):

Format	Amount	Collection/File Number	Photographer/Affiliation
Digital			
D-stretch			
Drone			
Color slides			
Color prints			
B&W prints			

Other Forms of Documentation (*insert details for all that apply*):

Format	Collection/File Number	Illustrator/Affiliation
Field Drawing		
Digital Drawing		
Tracing		

Documentation is on file at:
Assessor(s):
Affiliation:

Appendix B: Panel Form Discussion

The blank panel form in Appendix A is the one used by Sacred Sites Research (SSR) teams for recording rock art panels in New Mexico. Some states require the completion of specific supplemental forms, while other states have no required form and leave the choice of form to the recorder. The SSR form is relatively complicated because it requires information on the condition of the panel and its integrity and significance. These items can be omitted from a form created by the recorder and included elsewhere in the final project report.

The *site number* and *name* will be specific to the project, and the *date*, *time*, *weather*, and *temperature* are usually completed using short phrases like "sunny" or "partly cloudy" and an estimate of temperature and humidity. The latter data may not seem relevant, but rock art conservators are aware that a panel surface looks different at minus 5 degrees Fahrenheit than it does at 105 degrees Fahrenheit.

The *panel location* is usually a cliff face, rockshelter, or boulder, but sometimes petroglyphs occur on flat bedrock. The relationship of the panel to others can be useful when exploring relationships between figures. It is usually given as "XX meters east or right" (or a different direction) of another panel.

UTM data are often kept in a separate file and added to the form later. The *aspect*, or direction the panel is facing, is collected on site by holding a compass and standing in front of the panel, facing away. SSR recorders use a small compass, but the compass on smartphones is a good choice as it provides both degrees and direction. The *angle* refers to whether the panel face is vertical or sloping in or out at the base. The surface can have a variable angle, with one part vertical and another part sloping. In this instance, description may be warranted.

Recording the *rock type* is important. Rock art is most commonly found on limestone, basalt, and sandstone but can be found on other types of rock as well. If the rock type is sandstone, at some point the actual geological formation should be determined because some sandstones are more resistant to erosion, and older figures might be found on them.

The *panel size* is important, but determining its boundaries can be difficult because there is no one way to record it. Measuring the height and width of elements on the panel is one approach, but sometimes a panel surface consists of a flat chunk of the rock that frames the figures. In this instance, the height and width of this surface would be recorded.

The *height of the lowest and highest elements* on the panel can be useful. As a rule, the higher the figures are, the older they are, and although this is not uniformly true, it is important to know where the highest and lowest figures are. These are usually measured to ground surface, but sometimes it is to a ledge under the panel.

The *depth of deposits* covering a panel is also important. Inserting a pin flag into the dirt below a panel will usually offer information on soil depth.

Varnish cover is a relative estimate made by the recorder about how much manganese and iron is coating the figures on the panel. On some SSR projects, one person will make all the estimates to reduce the variability in estimates if several persons are involved. Since figures on the same panel can differ in the amount of varnish covering them, it is necessary to note this in the comments section.

The techniques used to make rock art are not always easy to identify. *Stipple pecking* leaves areas of the original rock varnish between the peck marks, whereas *solid pecking* removes these areas. There is often a debate about whether lines are *incised* (deeper) versus *scratched* (lighter), but experience in recording will help differentiate between the two types.

The techniques used to apply paint are also difficult to determine, and even the most experienced recorders are sometimes uncertain how a painting was made. *Brush strokes* are sometimes apparent, and *finger-applied paint* can be easier to recognize based on the width of the lines. *Dry paint* that was applied with crayons composed of rendered fat mixed with pigments is recognizable because the pigment does not fill the cracks or crevices in a rock surface as liquid paint does. *Charcoal lines*, which tend to skip over the low points in a surface, are often apparent for the same reason.

There is some debate about the best conditions for accurately determining paint color—in sun or in shade, with sunglasses on or off—because of the variability in individuals' perception of color. Nonetheless, SSR archaeologists use the *Munsell color system* because it provides a standard for determining and comparing paint colors, and it can be helpful when working with degrees of varnish cover.

Natural rock incorporation is an important feature to record because the connection between figures to cracks or natural rock protuberances is essential to defining the form of the images.

Superimposition is discussed in Step 8 in terms of its importance in determining whether one figure has been placed on top of another and, if so, can provide a clue to the relative age of both figures. A definitive decision is not always possible, but in the absence of a more reliable dating technique, an effort should be made to define placement of the figures.

It is important to provide short descriptions of *cultural features* found adjacent to the panel. Bedrock metates, mortars, and cupules are common near petroglyph panels. Rock shrines and rock-outlined fasting beds are usually described as part of the overall site data, but they can sometimes be directly associated with a panel.

Medicinal plants near panels are significant. At some sites there may be a correlation between tobacco and red paint that is important to note. If a recorder is unable to identify wild tobacco or other common medicinal plants, a smartphone connected to a plant identification app should be consulted.

The space provided for a *short description of panel and elements* is where the figures are briefly described and the measurements of several key figures are provided. This is straightforward if the panel has one or two figures, but panels with 20 or more figures can be complicated. SSR archaeologists usually write a few words about the figures and then wait until the panel drawings are completed before including the more detailed descriptions that will appear in the final report, which can also be cut and pasted into the panel form.

The *age estimation* section can be difficult to fill out because the age is often unknown, but the figures themselves can provide clues. For example, bows and arrows indicate a Formative time frame, whereas guns fit into the Historic period. Cultural affiliation is not usually known, but with experience it is possible to differentiate Basketmaker rock art from later Ancestral Puebloan types. In other panels, Crow horses can be differentiated from Blackfoot horses. Other similar pairings can provide information that can be noted on the panel form.

Judging *panel condition* requires some experience examining rock surfaces, but with time it is possible to recognize natural surface alterations. This section is not included on the forms provided by many other states, and recorders creating their own forms may prefer to omit it.

Wash zones are self-explanatory, but recognizing soluble versus insoluble mineral deposits on a panel can be challenging. Soluble minerals are, of course, going to dilute in water, but no one tests this on-site. A judgment is usually based on how hard or soft and loose the mineral crust is—insoluble being hard, and soluble so soft it rubs off easily.

Abrasion can occur when a tree branch rubs against a panel or when a human purposely tries to obliterate a figure. *Cleavage* results when cracks and slabs of the surface are about to break off or have broken off. *Dust* is easy to see. *Exfoliation* refers to areas of the rock surface that are flaking off, often containing parts of paintings, whereas *granulation* is a sugary type of erosion often caused by wind on sandstone.

Lichen is easily recognized, but it may be difficult to distinguish between the less common *fungi*, *mold*, and *algae*. Evidence of *animals* is usually obvious, particularly the nests of Cliff Swallows.

Graffiti and *vandalism* are, unfortunately, common at rock art sites and easy to recognize. Other forms of destruction may leave more subtle indications. Evidence of rock climbing, for example, is found in the presence of the chalk used by climbers to improve their grip. *Livestock damage* is extremely common, resulting from cattle and sheep rubbing against the panels as they seek shade.

A large portion of the third page of the form is devoted to information for the National Register of Historic Places. As such, a recorder could omit it from a form created for personal use. The first two queries, on *panel integrity* and *significance*, are closely related. The goal is to determine how the particular panel being recorded contributes to the significance of the site. Nearly all rock art is considered significant, but certain figures or groups of figures may exhibit a higher quality of execution; in such cases, the artist was more skilled at image-making than others, and that skill is often apparent in the design and workmanship of the panel. Noting a panel's significance is especially important for the National Register.

A point that has not been resolved by state historic preservation offices (SHPOs) is whether a faded painted panel has integrity if it is only completely visible in DStretch or another photographic enhancement technique. From a visual perspective at the site level, the panel appears to have little integrity, but the enhanced image retains considerable research potential. As rock art researchers increasingly rely on image enhancement software, it behooves SHPO archaeologists to discuss its prevalence and to establish some guidelines for its use.

The results of previous recording work at a site contribute greatly to work in the present. Previous records describing and perhaps including photos and drawings of the panels offer an opportunity to learn how the figures have changed through time. Research at a site is an ongoing process that benefits from the addition of more information to the panel form after workers leave the field. Once the recording team returns to the laboratory, a search of past records and photographic documentation should be pursued in libraries and curation facilities. A future researcher who visits the site as part of a new endeavor will find the panel forms invaluable, particularly if a full final report was not written and made available to other archaeologists.

References

Abel, Brent

1993 Proposed Investigations at Two Western Archaic Petroglyph Sites near Pecos, New Mexico. In *American Indian Rock Art*, Vol. 20, edited by Frank G. Bock, pp. 13–18. American Rock Art Research Association, San Miguel, California.

Adams, Ansel

1935 *Making a Photograph*. The Studio Publications, New York.

Albers, Patricia

2003 *The Home of the Bison: An Ethnographic and Ethnohistorical Study of Traditional Cultural Affiliations with Wind Cave National Park*. 2 vols. Report on file with the National Park Service, Wind Cave, South Dakota.

Andreae, Meinrat O., Abdullah Al-Amri, Claire M. Andreae, Maria Guagnin, Klaus Peter Jochum, Brigitte Stoll, and Ulrike Weis

2020 Archaeometric Studies on the Petroglyphs and Rock Varnish at Kilwa and Sadaka, Northern Saudi Arabia. *Arabian Archaeology and Epigraphy*. http://www.wileyonlinelibrary.com/journal.

Andreae, Meinrat O., and Tracey W. Andreae

2022 Archaeometric Studies on Rock Art at Four Sites in the Northeastern Great Basin of North America. *PLOS One* 7(1):e0263189.

Andreae, Meinrat, Tracey W. Andreae, Julie Francis, and Lawrence Loendorf

2023 Age Estimates for the Rock Art at the Rocky Ridge Site (Utah) Based on Archaeological and Archaeometric Evidence. *Journal of Archaeological Science Reports* 48:122.

Andrews, Thomas, and Jack Brink

2022 Using retroReveal as a Complement to DStretch for Enhancing Red Ochre Pictographs. Paper delivered at the American Rock Art Research Association 2022 Virtual Conference.

Bahn, Paul

1988 Comment on J. D. Lewis-Williams and T. A. Dowson, "The Signs of All Times: Entoptic Phenomena in Upper Paleolithic Art." *Current Anthropology* 29(2):217–218.

Basso, Keith

1996 *Wisdom Sits in Places: Landscape and Language Among the Western Apache.* University of New Mexico Press, Albuquerque.

Benson, L. V., E. M. Hattori, J. Southon, and B. Aleck

2013 Dating North America's Oldest Petroglyphs, Winnemucca Lake Subbasin, Nevada. *Journal of Archaeological Science* 40:4466–4476.

Boyd, Carolyn, and J. Phil Dering

2013 Rediscovering Ingredients in Paintings of the Pecos River Style. In *Painters in Prehistory: Archaeology and Art of the Lower Pecos Canyonlands*, edited by Harry J. Shafer, pp. 180–181. Trinity University Press, San Antonio, Texas.

Brady, Liam Michael, Jamie Hampson, and Inés Domingo Sanz

2017 Recording Rock Art: Strategies, Challenges, and Embracing the Digital Revolution. In *The Oxford Handbook of the Archaeology and Anthropology of Rock Art*, edited by Bruno David and Ian J. McNiven. https://doi.org/10.1093/oxfordhb.

Brown, David O., Byron Camino, and Mark D. Willis

2010 Algunas Observaciones a las Fortalezas Incas del Oeste Montañoso del Ecuador. *Revista del Patrimonio Cultural del Ecuador* 2:43–56. Instituto Nacional de Patrimonio Cultural, Quito.

Brumm, Asam, Adhi Agus Oktaviana, Basran Burhan, Budianto Hakim, Rustan Lebe, Jian-Xim Zhao, Priyatno Hadi Sulistyarto, Shinatria Adhityatama, Iwan Sumantri, and Maxime Aubert

2021 Oldest Cave Art Found in Sulawesi. *Sciences Advances* 7:1–12.

Castañeda, Amanda, Charles Koenig, Jerod Roberts, Victoria Roberts, Jay Franklin, Carolyn Boyd, and Karen Steelman

2019 Portable X-Ray Fluorescence Analysis of Red Linear Style Figures at 41VV1000. *Bulletin of the Texas Archaeological Society* 90:19–34.

Castañeda, Amanda, Lawrence Loendorf, and Julie Francis

2021 Rock Art Traditions at the Wold Ranch, Wyoming. In *American Indian Rock Art*, Vol. 47, edited by David A. Kaiser, Mavis Greer, and James D. Keyser, pp. 1–16. American Rock Art Research Association.

Cerrillo-Cuenca, E., and M. Sepulveda

2015 An Assessment of Methods for Digital Enhancement of Rock Paintings: The Rock Art from the Precordillera of Arica (Chile) as a Case Study. *Journal of Archaeological Science* 55:197–208.

Chippindale, C., and P. S. C. Taçon

1993 Two Old Painted Panels from Kakadu: Variation and Sequence in Arnhem Land Rock Art. In *Time and Space: Dating and Spatial Con-*

siderations in Rock Art Research: Papers of Symposia F and E, AURA Congress, Cairns 1992, edited by J. A. Steinbring, J. A. Watchman, P. Faulstich, and P. S. C Taçon, pp. 32–56. Occasional AURA Publication 8. Australian Rock Art Research Association, Melbourne.

Domingo, Inés, and Annalisa Chieli

2021 Characterizing the Pigments and Paints of Prehistoric Artists. *Archaeological and Anthropological Sciences* 13:196–226.

Domingo Sanz, Inés

2020 Rock Art Recording Methods From Traditional to Digital. In *Encyclopedia of Global Archaeology, Archaeology of Art* section, edited by Claire Smith, pp. 6351–6457. Springer, New York.

Dorn, Ronald

1997 A Change in Perception. *La Pintura* 23(2):10–11.

Fell, Barry

1976 *America B.C.: Ancient Settlers in the New World*. Pocket Books, New York.

Gerber, Creighton

2018 Digital Recording and Interpretation of Rock Art at Walnut Canyon National Monument. Master's thesis, Department of Anthropology, Northern Arizona University, Flagstaff, Arizona. https://openknowledge.nau.edu/id/eprint/5431/.

Gillette, Donna

2011 Cultural Markings on the Landscape: The PCN Pecked Curvilinear Nucleated Tradition in the Northern Coastal Ranges of California. PhD dissertation, Department of Anthropology, University of California, Berkeley.

Greer, Mavis

1995 Archaeological Analysis of Rock Art Sites in the Smith River Drainage of Central Montana. PhD dissertation, Department of Anthropology, University of Missouri, Columbia.

Greer, Mavis, and John Greer

2021 Furthering Our Understanding of Foothills Abstract Tradition Sites in Central Montana. *Archaeology of Montana* 62(1):37–69.

Greer, Mavis, John Greer, and James Keyser

2006 The Pros and Cons of Tracing Rock Art: The 2005 Season at Bear Gulch Pictographs, Montana. Paper presented at the 71st Annual Meeting of the Society for American Archaeology, San Juan, Puerto Rico.

Halifax, Joan

1982 *Shaman: The Wounded Healer.* The Crossroad, New York.

Hawkins, Seth C., and R. Bryan Simon
2021 Ten Myths about Medical Emergencies and Medical Kits. *Advances in Archaeological Practice* 9:23–33.
Hedges, Ken
1982 Phosphenes in the Context of Native American Rock Art. In *American Indian Rock Art* Vols. 7–8, edited by F. G. Bock, pp. 1–10. American Rock Art Research Association, El Toro, California.
Heizer, Robert F., and Martin A. Baumhoff
1962 *Rock Art of California and Eastern California*. University of California Press, Berkeley.
Henderson, J. W.
2002 Digitizing the Past: A New Procedure for Faded Rock Painting Photography. *Canadian Journal of Archaeology* 26(1):25–40.
Henshilwood, Christopher, Francesco d'Enrico, Karen L. van Niekerk, Laure Dayet, Alain Oueffelec, and Luca Pollarolo
2018 *An Abstract Drawing from the 73,000-Year-Old Levels at Blombos Cave, South Africa*. Nature Letter, Springer Nature Limited.
Hernbrode, Janine, and Peter Boyle
2016 Petroglyphs and Bell Rocks at Cocoraque Butte: Further Evidence of the Flower World Belief Among the Hohokam. In *American Indian Rock Art*, Vol. 49, edited by Ken Hedges, pp. 91–105. American Rock Art Research Association, Phoenix.
Hoffmann, D. L., C. Standish, M. Garcia Diez, P. B. Petitt, J. A. Zilhão, J. Alcolea-Gonzalez, P. Cantalejo-Duarte, et al.
2018 U-Th Dating of Carbonate Crusts Reveals Neanderthal Origin of Iberian Cave Art. *Science* 359:912–915.
Horowitz, M. J.
1964 The Imagery of Visual Hallucinations. *Journal of Nervous and Mental Disease* 38:513–523.
Hyman, Marian, and Marvin W. Rowe
1997a Plasma Extraction and AMS 14C Dating of Paintings. *Techne* 5: 61–70.
1997b Plasma-Chemical Extraction and AMS Radiocarbon Dating of Rock Paintings. In *American Indian Rock* Art, Vol. 23, edited by Steven M. Freers, pp. 1–9. American Rock Art Research Association, San Miguel, California.
Kenmotsu, Nancy, Leonard Kemp, and Lawrence Loendorf
2012 *Jornada Rockshelters as Special Places: Investigations of 13 Sites along the Otero Mesa Escarpment, Fort Bliss Military Reservation, Otero County, New Mexico*. Fort Bliss Cultural Resource Reports

Nos. 11–12 and 11–26. Environmental Division, Garrison Command, Fort Bliss, Texas.

Klüver, H.

1942 Mechanism of Hallucinations. In *Studies in Personality*, edited by Q. McNemar and M. A. Merrill, pp. 175–207. McGraw-Hill, New York.

Layton, Robert

2001 *Australian Rock Art: A New Synthesis*. Cambridge University Press, Cambridge, U.K.

Lewis-Williams, J. D., T. A. Dowson, Paul G. Bahn, Robert G. Bednarik, John Clegg, Mario Consens, Whitney Davis, et al.

1988 The Signs of All Times: Entoptic Phenomena in Upper Paleolithic Art. *Current Anthropology* 29(2):201–245.

Liebman, Matt, Chester Walker, and Jennie Sturm

2013 Mapping Archaeological Sites Using an Unmanned Aerial Vehicle. *Newsletter of the New Mexico Archeological Council*. Albuquerque.

Lins, Andrew, Beth Price, Ken Sutherland, and Tom Tague

2011 *Final Report on the Non-Invasive Analysis of Pictographs and on Analysis of Graffiti at the Hueco Tanks State Park and Historic Site*. Report on file with Texas State Parks and Wildlife Department, El Paso County, Texas.

Loendorf, Chris R., and Lawrence L. Loendorf

2013 Analyzing Red Pictographs with Portable X-ray Fluorescence. In *American Indian Rock Art*, Vol. 39, edited by William D. Hyder, pp. 143–150. American Rock Art Research Association, Glendale, Arizona.

Loendorf, Lawrence

2001 Rock Art Recording. In *Handbook of Rock Art Research*, edited by David S. Whitley, pp. 55–79. AltaMira, Walnut Creek, California.

2008 *Thunder and Herds: Rock Art of the High Plains*. Left Coast, Walnut Creek, California.

2010 Landscape and Painted Walls: Images in Place. In *Painting the Cosmos: Metaphor and Worldview in Images from the Southwest Pueblos and Mexico*, edited by Kelley Hays-Gilpin and Polly Schaafsma, pp. 19–40. Bulletin 67. Museum of Northern Arizona, Flagstaff.

2018 En Toto Pecked Petroglyphs. In *Dinwoody Dissected: Looking at the Interrelationships Between Central Wyoming Petroglyphs*, edited by Danny N. Walker, pp. 7–20. Wyoming Archaeological Society, Laramie.

Loendorf, Lawrence, and Stuart Conner

2020 Winter Solstice and Buffalo. *Archaeology in Montana* 61(1):53–65.

Loendorf, Lawrence, Myles R. Miller, Leonard Kemp, Laurie White, and Mark Willis

2013 *Rock Art at Seven Localities in the Southern Sacramento Mountains, Organ Mountains, and Otero Mesa on Fort Bliss*. Geo-Marine, Inc., El Paso, Texas. Historic and Natural Resources Report No. 1212. Submitted to Environmental Division, Fort Bliss Garrison Command, Fort Bliss, Texas.

Loendorf, Lawrence, Linda Olson, Stuart Conner, and J. Claire Dean

1998 *A Manual for Rock Art Documentation*. Printed and distributed by Department of Art, Minot State University, Minot, North Dakota.

Loendorf, Lawrence, and Linda Scott-Cummings

2016 Dates at Valley of the Shields: A Lesson for Northwestern Plains Archaeologists. *Archaeology in Montana* 7(2):1–10.

Loendorf, Lawrence, and Laurie White

2021 Buffalo-Human Transformational Figures on the Northern Plains. In *American Indian Rock Art*, Vol. 47, edited by David A Kaiser, Mavis Greer, and James D. Keyser, pp. 43–54. American Rock Art Research Association, Orem, Utah.

Loendorf, Lawrence, Laurie White, and Greg White

2012 *Rock Art Tracing at Castle Gardens: Site 48FR108, Fremont County, Wyoming*. Report submitted to the Bureau of Land Management, Lander, Wyoming.

Loendorf, Lawrence, Laurie White, Mark Willis, Paula Reynosa, and Rahman Abdullayev

2015 The Doña Ana Site (LA66667): Formative Period Abstract Rock Art. In *American Indian Rock Art*, Vol. 41, edited by James D. Keyser and David A. Kaiser, pp. 99–109. American Rock Art Research Association, Phoenix.

Loubser, Johannes

1997 The Use of Harris Diagrams in Recording, Conserving, and Interpreting Rock Paintings. *International Newsletter on Rock Art* 18:14–21.

2005 In Small Cupules Forgotten: Rock Markings, Archaeology, and Ethnography in the Deep South. In *Discovering North American Rock Art*, edited by Lawrence Loendorf, Christopher Chippindale, and David Whitley, pp. 131–160. University of Arizona Press, Tucson.

Mallery, Garrick

1886 Pictographs of the North American Indians: A Preliminary Paper. In *Fourth Annual Report of the Bureau of [American] Ethnology [for] 1882–'83*. Smithsonian Institution, Government Printing Office, Washington, DC.

1893 Picture-Writing of the American Indians. In *Tenth Annual Report of the Bureau of [American] Ethnology [for] 1888–'89*. 2 vols. Dover, New York, 1972.

Mark, Robert, and Evelyn Billo

2011 GigaPan Panoramas for Rock Art Panel Documentation: A Practical Guide. *Rock Art Research* 28:265–267.

Marymore, Leigh, and Marvin W. Rowe

2021 Bibliography of Rock Art Dating. *Rock Art Research* 38(1):101–116.

McHugh, John, John Lundwall, and Amy Larson

2021 Puebloan Ethnography to Explain the Function and Meaning of a Solar-Lunar Petroglyph at Fremont State Park. In *American Indian Rock Art*, Vol. 47, edited by David A. Kaiser, Mavis Greer, and James D. Keyser, pp. 173–185. American Rock Art Research Association, Orem, Utah.

Middleton, Emily, Geoffrey Smith, William Cannon, and Mary Ricks

2014 Paleoindian Rock Art: Establishing the Antiquity of Great Basin Carved Abstract Petroglyphs in the Northern Great Basin. *Journal of Archaeological Science* 43:21–30.

Miller, Myles R., Lawrence L. Loendorf, Tim B. Graves, and Mark Willis

2019 *Landscapes of Stone and Paint: Documentation and Analysis of 21 Rock Art Sites in Southeastern New Mexico*. Versar, Incorporated Report No. 863(a)p. Submitted to the Bureau of Land Management, Carlsbad, New Mexico, Field Office.

Miller, Myles R., Lawrence L. Loendorf, and Leonard Kemp

2012 *Picture Cave and Other Rock Art Sites on Fort Bliss*. Geo-Marine, Inc., El Paso, Texas. Historic and Natural Resources Report No. 13-36. Environmental Division, Fort Bliss Garrison Command, Fort Bliss, Texas.

Minick, David, and James Keyser

2022 Using retroReveal to Enhance Images at Montana Pictograph Sites. Paper delivered at the American Rock Art Research Association 2022 Virtual Meeting.

Mollard, Belinda C.

2020 Understanding a Ritual Landscape: An Investigation into the Rock Art of the Jornada Mogollon Region of the American Southwest. PhD dissertation, Department of Anthropology, University of Leicester, Leicester, England.

Morrison, Heather

2020 Portable X-Ray Fluorescence Compositional Analysis and Recording Techniques of Pictographs at Canyon de Chelly National

Monument. Master's thesis, Department of Anthropology, Northern Arizona University, Flagstaff.

Newman, Bonita, and Lawrence Loendorf

2005 Portable X-ray Fluorescence Analysis of Rock Art Pigments. *Plains Anthropologist* 50(195):277–283.

Poetschat, George, James Keyser, David Kaiser, Robin Harrower, and Anthony Farque

2010 Interpreting Cascadia Cave: An Upstream Struggle. In *American Indian Rock Art*, Vol. 36, edited by Ken Hedges, pp. 59–70. American Rock Art Research Association, Tucson, Arizona.

Popelka-Filcoff, Rachel S.

2006 Applications of Elemental Analysis for Archaeometric Studies: Analytical and Statistical Methods for Understanding Geochemical Trends in Ceramics, Ochre and Obsidian. PhD dissertation, Department of Chemistry, University of Missouri, Columbia.

Popelka-Filcoff, Rachel S., Elizabeth J. Miksa, J. David Robertson, Michael D. Glascock, and Henry Wallace

2008 Elemental Analysis and Characterization of Ochre Sources from Southern Arizona. *Journal of Archaeological Science* 35(3):752–762.

Ricks, M. F.

1995 A Survey and Analysis of Prehistoric Rock Art of the Warner Valley Region, Lake County, Oregon. PhD dissertation, Department of Systems Science, Portland State University, Portland, Oregon.

Robinson, David, Kelley Brown, Moira McMenemy, Lynn Dennany, Mathew Baker, Pamela Allan, Caroline Cartwright, et al.

2020 Datura Quids at Pinwheel Cave, California, Provide Unambiguous Confirmation of the Ingestion of Hallucinogens at a Rock Art Site. *Proceedings of the National Academy of Sciences of the United States of America* 117(49):31026–31037.

Rowe, Marvin

2001 Dating by AMS Radiocarbon Analysis. In *Handbook of Rock Art Research,* edited by David S. Whitley, pp. 139–166. AltaMira, Walnut Creek, California.

Rowe, Marvin W., Lawrence L. Loendorf, Myles R. Miller, and Karen L. Steelman

2021 Serpentine Bends Site #1: Radiocarbon Dating Prehistoric Soot and Associated Pictographs. *Journal of Archaeological Science Reports* 37 (June):102925.

Rowe, M. W., and K. L. Steelman

2003 Comment on "Some Evidence of a Date of First Humans to Survive in Brazil." *Journal of Archaeological Science* 30:1349–1351.

Ruskamp, John A., Jr.
2022 *Asiatic Echoes—The Identification of Ancient Chinese Pictograms in Pre-Columbian North American Rock Writing.* 3rd ed. https://www.asiaticechoes.org.

Russ, J. M., M. Hyman, H. J. Shafer, and M. W. Rowe
1990 Radiocarbon Dating of Prehistoric Rock Paintings by Selective Oxidation of Organic Carbon. *Nature* 348:710–771.

Schaafsma, Polly
1992 *Rock Art in New Mexico.* Museum of New Mexico Press, Santa Fe.
1994 Trance and Transformation in the Canyons: Shamanism and Early Rock Art on the Colorado Plateau. In *Shamanism and Rock Art*, edited by Solveig Turpin. Special Publication No. 1. Texas Rock Art Foundation, San Antonio.
2000 *Warrior, Shield, and Star: Imagery and Ideology of Pueblo Warfare.* Western Edge, Santa Fe, New Mexico.

Schaeffer, Bradley, and James Stamm
2020 Case Study of the Picture Rocks Sun Dagger, Plus a Review of the Intentionality of Sun Daggers. *Journal of Astronomical History and Heritage* 23(3):427–451.

Scott, Sara, Carl Davis, and J. M. Adovasio
2014 Radiocarbon Analysis of Four Perishable Artifacts from Ghost and Pictograph Caves, Montana. *Plains Anthropologist* 59(229): 70–95.

Siegel, R. K., and M. E. Jarvik
1975 Drug-Induced Hallucinations in Animals and Man. In *Hallucinations: Behavior, Experience, and Theory*, edited by R. K. Siegel and L. J. West, pp. 81–161. Wiley, New York.

Steelman, Karen, Jessica DeYoung, Charles Frederick, Charles Koenig, and Carolyn Boyd
2021 Geochemical Analyses at Eagle Cave, Texas: Radiocarbon Dating Oxalate Accretions Associated with Rock Paintings. In *American Indian Rock Art*, edited by David Kaiser, Mavis Greer, and James Keyser, pp. 227–240. American Rock Art Research Association, Orem, Utah.

Taçon, Paul S. C., and Christopher Chippindale
1998 An Archaeology of Rock-Art Through Informed and Formal Methods. In *The Archaeology of Rock-Art*, edited by Christopher Chippindale and Paul Taçon, pp. 1–10. Cambridge University Press, Cambridge, U.K.

Turpin, Solveig A.
1994 On a Wing and a Prayer: Flight Metaphors in Pecos River Pictographs. In *Shamanism and Rock Art in North America*, edited by

Solveig A. Turpin, pp. 73–102. Special Publication 1. Texas Rock Art Foundation, San Antonio, Texas.

Velliky, Elizabeth, and Rudy Reimer

2013 Rock Paintings of the Squamish Valley, British Columbia: Geochemical Analysis of Pigments Using Portable X-ray Fluorescence Spectrometry pXRF. In *American Indian Rock Art* 39:131–142. Edited by William Hyder. American Rock Art Research Association, San Jose, California.

Waller, Steven

1993 Sound and Rock Art. *Nature* 363:401.

Welsh, Peter, and Ronald Dorn

1997 Critical Analysis of Petroglyph Radiocarbon Ages from Coa, Portugal, and Deer Valley, Arizona. In *American Indian Rock Art*, Vol. 23, edited by Frank Bock, pp. 11–24. American Rock Art Research Association, San Miguel, California.

Whitley, David

1996 *A Guide to Rock Art Sites in Southern California and Southern Nevada.* Mountain Press, Missoula, Montana.

Whitley, David S., and Lawrence L. Loendorf

2005 Rock Art Analysis. In *Handbook of Archaeological Methods*, vol. 2, edited by Herbert Maschner and Christopher Chippindale, pp. 919–973. AltaMira, Walnut Creek, California.

Willis, Mark D., and Andrea Jalandoni

2011 *The Pictographs of the Rock Islands of Koror, Palau: Advanced Enhancement and 3D Modeling at Five Sites for UNESCO.* Report submitted to the Ministry of Community and Cultural Affairs, Palau.

Winter, Joseph

2000 *Tobacco Use by Native North Americans: Sacred Smoke and Silent Killer.* Civilization of American Indian Series. University of Oklahoma Press, Norman.

Wylie, Alison

1989 Archaeological Cables and Tacking: The Implications of Practice for Bernstein's Options Beyond Objectivism and Relativism. *Philosophy of Science* 19:1. https://spinoff.nasa.gov/Spinoff2012//cg.4.html.

Zarzycka, Sandra, Todd Surovell, Madeline Mackie, Spencer Pelton, Robert Kelley, Paula Goldberg, Janet Dewey, and Meghan Kent

2019 Long-Distance Transport of Red Ocher by Clovis Foragers. *Journal of Archaeological Science Reports* 25:519–529.

Index

Locators in italics indicate figures or material in the front matter.